"The name of the Lord is a strong tower;
the righteous run to it and are safe."
~Proverbs 18:10

PREPARE!

FOR THE END-TIME HARVEST

DON FINTO

FOREWORD BY
TOD MCDOWELL

CALEB
PUBLICATIONS
NASHVILLE, TENNESSEE

All Scripture quotations, unless otherwise indicated, are taken from the Holy Bible, New International Version® Copyright © 1973, 1978, 1984 by International Bible Society. Used by permission of Zondervan Publishing House. All rights reserved.

Publication date: March 2015
Print: ISBN: 978-0-9861088-0-8
eBook: ISBN: 978-0-9861088-1-5
ePub: ISBN: 978-0-9861088-2-2

Library of Congress Control Number: 2015933764

1. Preparation 2. Last Days 3. End-Time 4. Harvest 5. Deception 6. Religion 7. Jesus 8. Christianity I. Finto, Don II. Prepare!

PREPARE! may be purchased at special quantity discounts. Resale opportunities are available for churches, donor programs, fund raising, book clubs, or educational purposes for churches, congregations, schools and universities. For more information contact tod@calebpublications.org

Caleb Publications
P.O. Box 493, Thompson's Station, TN 37179
(615) 790-3616

Caleb Publications Speakers Bureau: Have Don Finto or Tod McDowell speak at your church, fundraiser or special event.
For information call 615) 790-3616 or email tod@calebpublications.org

Cover and Interior Design by:
Birdsong Creative, Nashville, TN ~ www.birdsongcreative.com
Edited by Anne Severance

Printed in the United States of America

Publishing Consultant: Mel Cohen of Inspired Authors Press LLC
Publisher: Caleb Publications
PREPARE! Website: www.calebpublications.org

PRAISE FOR
PREPARE!

"Who better to guide our walk with the Lord than a godly man who has stayed the course for over eight decades? Don Finto may be in his senior years, but I have seen firsthand his vigor and passion for Jesus as he continues the race and finishes well. In his new book *PREPARE!* Don's writing reflects his true heart for the body of Jesus. There are dark days ahead for some of us, but when we join with wisdom, prayer and integrity, we can respond correctly even in times of unjust suffering. I hope you study the deep truths in this honest look at what it means to walk uprightly, and fulfill the purposes of God for your own life."

HEIDI G. BAKER, PHD
Co-Founder and Director, Iris Global

"*PREPARE!* is the impassioned battle-cry of a seasoned warrior that will help you fight and win your coming battles. *PREPARE!* is the meticulously charted course of a trusted sea captain that will help you successfully navigate the storm-tossed waters of change that are upon us all."

STEVE BERGER
Pastor, Grace Chapel, Leipers Fork, TN

"Jesus Himself promised to send 'prophets and wise men and scribes' to alert people to events about to occur. I'm convinced that Don Finto is one of those messengers, not just with the spoken words of prophecy, but as a scribe, having written these things for all of us in this book. A wise person will listen and take heed."

PAT BOONE
Singer, actor, writer

"I wish that every young leader would heed the wisdom and zeal that Don Finto pours out on the pages of this book. In a time with so much confusion, this book comes as a clarion call on how we ought to live now and in the days ahead! Young leaders, let us soak up the words of this time-tested spiritual father and truly live prepared lives!"

ANDY BYRD
School of the Circuit Rider Fire and Fragrance Ministries

"The words on these pages will inspire and ignite fresh fire in hearts everywhere. *PREPARE!* to be encouraged as well as challenged!"

CANDY CHRISTMAS
CEO/Founder, The Bridge, Inc., Nashville, TN

"*PREPARE!* comes at just the right time to encourage the followers of Jesus to 'prepare' with confidence and clarity. Don is a true 'Caleb' who calls us to an overcoming faith that refuses to bow to the giants of fear and discouragement. He prepares you with hope that the Body of the Messiah is about to enter her finest hour, despite the tribulations that lie ahead."

JAY COMISKEY
Vice President, CBN

"*PREPARE!* is a faith-building, much-needed reminder of the days ahead and the promise that fear has no place in the believer's life."

JEFF DOLLAR
Pastor, Grace Center, Franklin, Tennessee

"In words clear and profound, Don calls the people of God to understand the days in which we live, and to live them in full faith, courage and power. With so many cultural distractions —and so many prophetic messages—coming at us from so many directions, we must hear the sure voice of the Holy Spirit like never before. Don gives us not only a biblically-grounded road map to live adventurously in the end time, but a lifetime of his personal 'wisdom discoveries' distilled down to core truths."

STEVE FRY
President, Messenger Fellowship

"Some say with age comes maturity. In Don Finto's case, with advancing years comes red-hot zeal! This dear papa in the faith is one of the keenest, most energetic 'straight shooters' you will ever meet. This book you hold in your hand is a stick of dynamite that might just blow the body of Christ out of lethargy and passivity and act as a wake-up call into reality. The only thing missing in this book is a warning label. Warning: Contents will cause a fire to burn in your heart!"

JAMES GOLL
Encounters Network & Prayer Storm

"Using his unique combination of prophetic vision, pastoral compassion and paternal wisdom, 'Papa Don'—as he is lovingly called by those privileged to know him—has crafted a manual for these 'last days' in which we live. No 'doomsday' tome, this work warns and awakens, exhorts and inspires, provoking holy fear and producing Godly hope!"

MARTY GOETZ
Messianic Psalmist & Worship Leader

"*PREPARE!*" is an absolute must read for such a time as this! Sounding an alarm to make ready a Bride for the return of the Jealous Bridegroom! Body of Messiah, get ready for the soon return of Yeshua and His rule and reign with righteousness and justice! This book inspires hope, encourages, challenges, and strengthens you to overcome like the Lamb has overcome!"

SAMAA HABIB
Former Muslim and Author, Face to Face with Jesus!

"As usual, Don's writing is to the point, bringing complex topics 'down' home, where anyone can relate to it in a personal way. While some write about how to be successful, and others write about the difficulties, Don writes how to be successful in the midst of the difficulties. The book is real, practical, and simple—which in itself is no simple task. Don shows you how to face a disastrous situation that looks like a tidal wave, and then shows you how to ride a 'surfboard' of victorious faith, rising above the circumstances."

ASHER INTRATER
Jerusalem, Israel

"*PREPARE!* is passionate, clear, and a great corrective to the squishy, feckless type of Christianity that we sometimes see in the West."

DANIEL JUSTER
Tikkun International, Restoration from Zion

"The Scripture says, 'A word aptly spoken is like apples of gold in settings of silver' (Pr. 25:11). *PREPARE!* is such a word for this season in the church, given to us by a 'father in the faith' whose life is the embodiment of this message. As one blessed to be 'fathered' by Don for the past two decades, I can promise you—the return for the time invested in reading this book will be great."

DAVID MCQUEEN
Pastor, Beltway Park Baptist, Abilene, TX

"This is my kind of book. It causes courage and hope to arise—a vital message from God's heart—as darkness falls on humanity. Don's passion to shine in these tumultuous, threatening last days is contagious. May you catch it and live it!"

EITAN SHISHKOFF
Tents of Mercy Network, Israel

"I call him 'Papa Don.' And no one, outside my immediate family, has had a greater impact on me. I have walked with, listened to, been mentored by, discipled by, and taught by this Godly man for over half my life. His love of people and dedication to God has been an inspiration to me and to countless others. Don has always had a keen sense for delivering just the right message at just the right time. *PREPARE!* is that kind of book."

MICHAEL W. SMITH
Singer/Songwriter

TABLE OF
CONTENTS

We must learn to listen to the Calebs and Joshuas of our generation—those who see the dangers, but know that God will be victorious—rather than listening to the ten spies who only see the giants.

Jesus told us that wickedness and righteousness would ripen side by side as we approach the end. We are to shine most brilliantly in the deepening darkness.

Israel experienced the horror of the first plagues, but was protected from the last plagues. John's Revelation describes the ultimate Passover, a time when we experience some of the horror, but then are protected if we are faithful to God's ways.

Never does Scripture tell us that we will escape tribulation, but that we should be prepared for times of tribulation, even The Great Tribulation.

God's wrath is never for believers.

Jesus and the apostles spoke of signs that would announce the season of His return. Those signs are increasing in our generation.

Both Jesus and His disciples warn that in the last days, deceit will abound, that "even from your own number" men will arise who distort the truth. Only faithfulness to God's Word will keep us from such deception.

What if the rapture is simply a welcoming committee rising to escort the King of Kings back to Jerusalem where He will reign for a thousand years in an era of unprecedented peace?

FOREWORD

I met Don Finto on February 4, 2005. He was sitting in the courtyard of the Visitors' Center of Youth With A Mission's (YWAM) largest training campus in Kona, Hawaii. He wasn't what I expected. He was good-looking and energetic, with a smile that made me feel accepted and comfortable immediately. His youthful exuberance and child-like humility drew me in. What made this man tick? What was it that caused such life and love to emanate from him?

As I sat down on the plastic chair, my mind flashed back to three days earlier. My phone had rung with a call from Australia, a number I didn't recognize. I was on the 33rd day of a 40-day fast, seeking keys to global revival. I had been in YWAM, the world's largest mission organization, for thirteen years, serving on the president's council, teaching in their School of Biblical Studies, leading outreach teams all over the world, and had recently begun a worship and intercession team called IGNITE.

But I was yearning for more of God's heart. I had withdrawn from ministry for a season so that I could spend my days in fasting and prayer. I met with my IGNITE team once a week, but had asked not to be called unless there was some unusual need. The phone call was, therefore, unexpected.

"Hello, Tod!" came the voice on the other end of the line as I reluctantly took the call. "Tod, I love what you are doing, and totally agree with the revelation the Lord is giving you. Worship and intercession are indeed core essentials for world revival, but I believe you are missing a piece. You need to get the 'Israel piece.'"

Stunned, I pressed my caller for more.

"You need to read this book by Don Finto, *Your People Shall be My People*," she said.

"Interesting," I responded. "I actually have that book. It was given to me in Singapore when John Dawson became president of YWAM."

I thanked my friend for the call and hung up the phone, pondering, praying.

What is this all about, Lord? Why would she feel the necessity to call? Don't I know more about world revival than she? Yet I trust her as an intercessor (Her two children were a part of our IGNITE team). *Lord, what's going on?*

Still a bit shaken by the whole encounter, I received another phone call about an hour later, this time from one of the school leaders over which I had oversight. "Tod, please excuse me for calling," she said, "but I really believe the Lord wanted me to call. We have a guest speaker on campus this week, and I felt that you may want to get with him. He has a free day on Friday. His name is Don Finto."

Now I am doubly stunned.

And so, on this Friday morning at eleven o'clock, I am sitting with Don as he is giving me his best Power Point for believing that our relationship with Israel and the Jewish people is a key for world revival. What he was saying was interesting, but not necessarily life-changing until he hit Romans 11:12.

"If their [Jewish] transgression means riches for the world, and their [Jewish] loss means riches for the Gentiles [the nations], how much greater riches will their fullness bring?"

"Wait a minute!" I said, as that verse sprang alive within me. "I believe there is something here that I need. Would you pray for me?"

Tears welled up in my eyes as I knelt, Don kneeling beside me. Soon I was facedown weeping, asking God to speak to me and tell me what was happening. All I heard was, "You are married to the Jewish people."

Married to the Jewish people? Is Rachel Jewish? Lord, what are you trying to tell me?

Then I realized that if God is in covenant with the Jewish people, then I also am in covenant with the Jewish people.

Later on that Friday evening, we were in a campus dinner where Don was present before returning to Nashville the next day. I introduced him to Rachel and the children, and we spent perhaps fifteen minutes together. We were both impacted by the time together, but neither of us had any expectancy of ever being together again.

One month later, I got a call from Israel. It was Don. "Tod, I just stepped out of a meeting with my Israeli brothers here in Israel. The prophetic brother among us looked at me and said, 'You've met this young man. He has your DNA. He has your ambassadorial anointing. You are supposed to be walking together during the next season.' I think he's talking about you, Tod. I believe we are to be walking together for the next season.

I am not sure what that means. You live in Hawaii. I live in Nashville, but why don't you and Rachel pray about it and call me back?"

Two days later, after talking with trusted counselors, some of whom knew Don, we called back. "We don't know what this means either, but the answer is, 'Yes.'" And so it was that almost ten years ago, we began a spiritual father/son relationship, traveling together—to England, Turkey, Egypt, Korea, Africa, Europe, as well as points in the US. Over seven years ago, we moved to Nashville. I am now the Director of the Caleb Company that Don started in 1997. He is like a father to me. We talk or see each other almost daily: praying, ministering, traveling, and strategizing together. It is a great privilege to partner with Don in building the kingdom through "equipping God's people with his heart and purpose for Israel and the nations" through Caleb Company. My marriage, family and personal walk with Jesus have been profoundly strengthened through walking with Don.

"PREPARE!" is the word for today. Don writes from the heart. His literary astuteness and biblical accuracy give this book a solid foundation. Living out his faith for over seventy years gives Don a unique authority and perspective on knowing what is important to "finish strong." Don's passion is contagious. His encouragement goes deep into one's mind, heart, and soul. This book will transform those who read with open hearts. Your spirit will be awakened with fresh faith. The warnings presented are clear and practical. The goal of this book is application. It is written with clarity of thought so the reader is able easily to integrate truth into life.

A passion for revival emanates through the pages. Hope infuses the end-time realities that are objectively presented. I have heard Don speak these messages to diverse audiences, each time watching as a Holy fear of the Lord settles on the hearers, like light bulbs are turned on. Clarity comes to many of the "gray" areas that many Christian leaders don't attempt to address in our day of "political correctness."

Don primarily writes this book, but my heart pulsates with the same desire. To see God's people equipped to be fruitful and powerful in these last days. Great evil is ripening in our world, but the good news is that great righteousness, revival, and awakening are also ripening. God's power is being released throughout the world. Join with Don and me on this God-pilgrimage, and receive the challenge to press into the light and shine most brilliantly in the deepening world darkness.

Our best days are ahead.

~**Tod McDowell**
Director, Caleb Company
Nashville, Tennessee

ACKNOWLEDGMENTS

Scripture continually calls us to "enter His gates with thanksgiving" (Ps. 100:4), and to bring our prayers and petitions to God "with thanksgiving" (Phil. 4; see also Col. 4:2). I have to be one of the most blessed people alive! Not only am I forgiven, counted righteous, and have an inheritance that is eternal, but I am blessed with a faithful wife of over sixty-two years, with children and grandchildren who love us and love each other, and with an extended family that reaches around the world.

Our Caleb family—I smile every time I am among them or even think about them—are scattered among the nations. They are passionate, Godly, prayerful, worshiping, hungry disciples of Jesus. Without them, I could never become who God has called me to be. They challenge, inspire, and encourage me. Thank you, all of you!

What can I say to the Lord for having brought Tod McDowell and me together? As Eitan Shishkoff told me, "You've traveled with many young men through the years. This is the one you were looking for!" In many ways, he was right. In the spring of 2005, God prophetically/supernaturally brought Tod into my life as a spiritual son, a general in the Lord's army, destined to lead His people forward into strength and power as we hasten toward the return of the King. He has expressed himself personally in the Foreword and in the chapter on listening to the Holy Spirit, but our hearts have become so interwoven that he is a part of every chapter. Thank you, Tod, Rachel, Mandy, Micah, Makai'o and Moses, for being obedient when God called you to leave the surfing waves of Hawaii and settle into Nashville during the heat wave in the summer of 2007.

I would be arrogantly remiss if I pretended to have written without the aid of Anne Severance's edits. She taught and continues to teach me how to put into words what my heart is trying to say. She is a gentle, humble, gifted woman of God who continually challenges and motivates me. Thank you, Anne, for being there for the *Your People* book, the *God's Promise* book, and now *PREPARE!*

INTRODUCTION

Seven words...one sentence...changed the way I look at the future.

"Let both grow together until the harvest."

Those seven words from Jesus' own mouth (see Matt. 13:30), describing the parallel increase of both wickedness and righteousness in the world, have convinced me that the opening phrases from Dickens's *The Tale of Two Cities* are the perfect description of days just ahead: "It was the best of times, it was the worst of times, it was the age of wisdom, it was the age of foolishness, it was the epoch of belief, it was the epoch of incredulity, it was the season of Light, it was the season of Darkness...."

The darkest time in all of history as well as the most brilliant for the people of God lies before us. It is the exciting possibilities of this next season that compelled me to write this book.

While the quotation by Charles Dickens comes from a classic English novel of the eighteenth century, the seven words of Jesus are quoted from one of His parables in the Bible—one of those "the-kingdom-of-heaven-is-like" stories that speak to our day.

"'Why do you speak to the people in parables?'" the disciples asked Jesus (Matt. 13:10).

"'The knowledge of the secrets of the kingdom of heaven has been given to you, but not to them,'" was His reply (v. 11). In other words, "I speak in parables so that those who want to know truth will find it, but those who are not interested will pass over my remarks as meaningless."

In one parable, Jesus told the story of a farmer who sowed wheat in his field. During the night, an enemy came and sowed weeds among the wheat. As the seedlings grew, the plants looked so similar that the servants were unaware of what had happened. But as the harvest neared, the mixture was manifested, and the servants asked the farmer, "Do you want us to go and pull them [the weeds] up?" (v. 28).

"'No,' he answered, 'because while you are pulling the weeds, you may root up the wheat with them.'" Now listen again to these seven critical words: "Let both grow together until the harvest" (vv. 29, 30).

This book is all about wheat and weeds growing together until the harvest—wickedness and righteousness maturing side by side until the end—the most evil as well as the Godliest generation of all time sharing the world stage just prior to Jesus' return.

Jesus' intriguing words led me to listen closely to His answer when the disciples came to Him later and asked for the interpretation of the parable (vv. 36–43). His words directed me to the prophets, whom Jesus often quoted, as well as to teaching from the apostles, especially John's Revelation about the end of our age when "the harvest of the earth is ripe" (14:15).

Several years ago, I became captivated by Jesus' words in Luke 21 concerning the destruction of Jerusalem, the scattering of Jewish people among the nations, and Gentile domination of that city until their time had come to a close, and Jewish people would regain control of the city. The revelation that began coming to me inspired me to write *Your People Shall Be My People* and *God's Promise and The Future of Israel*. The thesis of both books has to do with the timing of God in our generation, a time in which Jewish people by the tens of thousands are beginning to believe that Yeshua/Jesus is indeed the promised Messiah and the corresponding awakening of faith among the nations that Jesus is not only Israel's Messiah, but the World Redeemer.

My own personal awakening led me to take a harder look at Israel's prophets, as well as the end-time messages of Jesus and the apostles.

Many believe that Spirit-empowered believers will be "taken away" before our enemy launches his last great assault. I see many reasons for rejecting that theory and the need to expend our energy preparing to weather the coming storms and shine most brilliantly during the world's darkest hour.

I am learning to trust the Word of God even when I do not understand it. Another verse I've quoted for years and believe most of the time is Romans 8:28. I have read these words in various versions just to be sure I'm not misreading Paul's core thought.

"And we know that in all things God works for the good of those who love him, who have been called according to his purpose" (NIV).

"We are assured and know that [God being a partner in their labor] all things work together and are [fitting into a plan] for good to and for those who love God and are called according to [His] design and purpose" (Amplified).

"And we know that God causes all things to work together for good to those who love God, to those who are called according to His purpose" (NASB).

All things!

All!

For good!

Not for everyone, but for those who love the Lord and are called of Him.

One of my close friends once preached a sermon entitled "The Most Difficult Verse in the Bible to Believe." It was Romans 8:28! I happened to be in the congregation that day and was surprised at the verse he had chosen. Yet I found myself immediately agreeing with him.

Even though I have quoted the verse almost my entire life, I still find it impossible to grasp except that I know God is always right. He never misses a beat. No matter how grim the situation, how intense the suffering, no matter how evil the consequences, He finds a way to mold all the circumstances for good for those of us who have embraced Him as our Leader.

In looking back over my own life, I see how true Paul's words are. I would never have chosen for my own father to abandon the family, my mother to die, and for me to experience sexual molestation from a trusted preacher cousin as a way of drawing me into the heart of God. But I realize that God used the confusion of that time and Godly grandparents to compel me to know Him even at an early age.

How could I have known that God would use that childhood trauma to make me more desperate for Him and more willing to follow Him? But God knew the call He wanted to place on my life and was using every circumstance to mold me into that destiny. My role was to keep loving Him and trusting Him.

Now, a few years later and after a lifetime of learning to believe this verse, I am about to tell you of some things that are predicted in Scripture that do not sound good at all. Still, I completely believe that God will work all the bad stuff that is coming in the future for our good if we will simply hang onto Him and trust Him.

Jesus' seven words have motivated me to challenge the people of God to become radical, God-empowering, miracle-working, people-rescuing followers of Jesus as the final harvest nears. So join me on this pilgrimage. Don't be afraid when you read about what we will be facing. Always remember Romans 8:28. And in case you should be tempted to forget along the way, I'll keep reminding you.

LISTEN TO THE RIGHT REPORT!

Then Caleb silenced the people before Moses and said,
"We should go up and take possession of the land, for we can certainly do it."
~Numbers 13:30

Recently in Nashville, word spread through the Christian community that two strategic films were being previewed at one of our local theaters. The films were to give helpful, behind-the-scene depictions of world events. I made my plans to attend.

On the night of the showing, the small theater was packed to capacity with representatives from the believing community, many of them friends of mine from a variety of congregations across the city. An air of anticipation filled the room as we settled in for the evening.

Not long into the showing of the first film, I began to feel a certain discomfort. Everything being communicated seemed to be true, but the "God factor" was missing. The film was a well-documented account of enemy activity and of plans for world domination, including the frightening inroads currently being made into our own nation.

Earlier in the day, I had been reading of the unprecedented Godly underground awakening in the very nations that were being described in the film. Yet nothing of those revivals was being reported.

By the time the first film concluded and the host came to the podium to introduce the second film, my uneasiness had increased. I don't recall his exact words, but I know what he seemed to be saying: "Over fifty years ago, Nazism threatened the entire world, but we defeated it. Then the dread of communism was upon us, but that, too, has fallen. Now we are faced with an even more insidious enemy. Radical Islam is encroaching on our communities, our schools, and our government. If this evil is not defeated, our country will become engulfed in a sea of mass terrorism."

As the second film began, I discreetly made my way to the exit. I had been listening to the report of the ten spies. Why was there no mention of the "God factor," the great advances for the gospel that were being made in the midst of the darkness? Where were the voices of Caleb and Joshua? In retrospect, I should have been one of those voices. I could have encouraged people to stay strong, no matter what the future holds.

Not long after this experience, another film was advertised for the same theater. Because of my acquaintance with those sponsoring the showing, I was present. The depiction was an end-time movie in which believers were being persecuted—even to death—but the story was saturated with what I call "but-God" stories. Even though I left the theater that night knowing that we could be entering a time of great persecution, I was encouraged. The strength and faith of believers was evident in the lives of those depicted.

THE CALEB AND JOSHUA VISION

Every Sunday school student knows the story.

The journey from Horeb, the area around Sinai, to Kadesh Barnea in the southern desert of Israel, was an eleven-day trip (see Deut. 1:2).

But that journey lasted forty years!

Why?

Because the nation listened to the reports of the ten spies, not to those of Caleb and Joshua.

Twelve men, among them Caleb and Joshua, were given the assignment of exploring the land promised to them by God and to bring back a report to Moses and the children of Israel. "Go up through the Negev and on into the hill country. See what the land is like and whether the people who live there are strong or weak, few or many. What kind of land do they live in? Is it good or bad? What kind of towns do they live in? Are they unwalled or fortified? How is the soil? Is it fertile or poor? Are there trees on it or not? Do your best to bring back some of the fruit of the land" (Num. 13:17–20).

For forty days, the twelve men faithfully followed instructions, observing the cities of the region and their inhabitants. At the end of this time, the spies brought back pomegranates and figs, along with a huge cluster of grapes, so heavy that it had to be carried by two men.

> Only Caleb and Joshua figured the "God factor" into the equation.

All twelve saw the same things, but their accounts to Moses and the leaders of Israel were significantly different. Only Caleb and Joshua figured the "God factor" into the equation. They remembered the promises and they believed God. The other ten spies described only what they saw with their natural eyes, even at times exaggerating the danger in order to sway the crowd.

"The people who live there are powerful, and the cities are fortified and very large," the ten reported. "We even saw descendants of Anak there. They are stronger than we" (v. 28, 31).

True. Factually accurate.

"The land we explored devours those living in it. All the people we saw there are of great size….We seemed like grasshoppers in their eyes, and we looked the same to them" (vv. 32–33).

Stretching truth to make the point!

"The cities are large, with walls up to the sky" (Deut. 1:28).

I don't think so. Over the top!

Caleb and Joshua were of an opposite spirit (see Num. 14:24). They saw the same thing, but judged differently. "We should go up and take possession of the land, for we can certainly do it," they implored (13:30). "The land we passed through and explored is exceedingly good. If the LORD is pleased with us, he will lead us into that land, a land flowing with milk and honey, and will give it to us. Only do not rebel against the LORD. And do not be afraid of the people of the land, because we will swallow them up. Their protection is gone, but the LORD is with us. Do not be afraid of them" (14:7–9).

DAYS OF THE GIANTS

The church is reliving the days of the giants. The circumstances around us are bewildering and foreboding. Two voices are dominant. One is the voice of fear that describes walled cities and giants. The other is the beckoning of God to a life of faith and victory over every enemy.

"What are we going to do?" asks the first voice. "We are in total moral decay. Over half of our marriages end in divorce. More and more of our young people are living together outside of marriage. Homosexuality is on the rise. Abortion statistics are staggering. Infanticide and euthanasia are on the horizon. Natural disasters are increasing. The price of oil is making normal living impossible. Bankruptcies are skyrocketing. Our leaders are no longer dependable. Our school systems are being infiltrated with textbooks that have rewritten history and advocate for godless lifestyles. Our nation is out from under the protection of God. Even the church is filled with greed, pride, and immorality."

Two voices are dominant, the voice of fear and the voice of faith.

These are accurate descriptions, but if we stop with these reports, we will not hear the voice of the Holy Spirit.

Is the world economy in danger? Yes.

Is terrorism rampant? Yes.

Are natural disasters intensifying? Is greed controlling the world? Are people of God being persecuted, imprisoned, and even executed for their faith? Yes. Yes. Yes.

But there is another side of the story.

In the midst of the deepening darkness, great light is appearing. Nations long held in bondage are hearing of the freedom that comes from the Jewish Messiah who has become Redeemer of all the nations. The greatest revival in history is upon us.

FEARLESS FAITH

Our own nation has for decades manifested a thin veneer of Christian faith. Such superficial Christianity is not adequate for the future.

But there is a rising body of Holy Spirit-empowered believers who have accepted not only the first two phrases of John's vision regarding power over the enemy: "They overcame him by the blood of the lamb and by the word of their testimony" (Rev. 12:11), but have also embraced that third phrase: "They did not love their lives so much as to shrink from death."

A proverbial expression from the early centuries of faith states, "The blood of the martyrs is the seed of the kingdom." No power of hell can defeat believers who are sold out to the Lord.

A recent report from a group of believers in the Middle East tells of thirteen people baptized to proclaim their allegiance to Jesus, their newly found Savior. Within two weeks, eleven of them were dead – honor killings by families who would not tolerate other family members forsaking the family religion.

Yet this report is from one of the countries where faith in Jesus is advancing with amazing speed. Great persecution often brings in an even greater harvest of souls.

"LET THEM KILL ME!"

I recall my only visit to China. The year was 1989, soon after the Beijing uprising that took the lives of hundreds if not thousands of young people in Tiananmen Square. Our group had traveled to Hong Kong, making repeated trips across the border into Guangzhou, always loaded with Bibles hidden in our luggage and praying to get through the checkpoint undetected. On one particular day, we flew from Guangzhou to Beijing, with multiple suitcases filled with Bibles that were to be distributed to underground church pastors. Arriving after midnight in Beijing, the airport had closed, so we were able to grab our luggage and head to the hotel.

The following morning, we set out to take the Bibles to the home of "Sister Mabel." She greeted us with great joy and ushered us into her tiny apartment. One whole wall was piled high with Bibles and study materials, waiting to be delivered to pastors who would be risking their lives to receive them.

"Aren't you afraid to keep all these Bibles so clearly visible in your apartment?" one of our group asked Sister Mabel.

"What can they do to me?" she answered with a shrug. "I've been in prison. Let them kill me. I'll only see Jesus more quickly."

Sister Mabel's work is still thriving though she has long since gone to be with the Lord. One of the young men who used to go to Sister Mabel's apartment to collect her Bibles and take them to pastors in the underground church movement was the son of Peter Xu, who today leads a network of house churches numbering into the millions. Peter, Enoch Wang, and Brother Yun, current Chinese leaders with whom we have recently visited, have endured a total of almost forty years in prison for their faith. They estimate that there are now 170 million believers in China, most of them in the house church movements.

FAITH INVOLVES RISK

During the 1920s, long before the great upsurge of believers in their nation, the "Back to Jerusalem" vision was born in the hearts of a few of China's believers. They *saw* 100,000 missionaries taking the gospel to the Buddhism of Southeast Asia, through the Hindu strongholds of northern India, and then finally flourishing in the Muslim nations of central Asia all the way to the Middle East and Israel. They knew that these men and women of God would be risking their lives to bring the gospel, but they were listening to the Caleb/Joshua voice of the Holy Spirit, rather than to the fears of man.[1]

In 1995, Rolland and Heidi Baker[2] went to Mozambique, Africa. They had no contacts and no money, but they had a vision. Mozambique was one of the poorest nations on earth and had been ravaged by almost thirty years of civil war. In the last nineteen years, the Bakers and their co-workers have poured out their lives for the poor, preached the gospel of Jesus, and cared for thousands of children, widows, single mothers, and others in need. Like Paul, they have experienced shipwrecks, stones and curses being hurled at them, sleepless nights, hunger, life-threatening diseases, and more, but they have also found those closing verses in Mark's gospel to be true: "The Lord worked with them and confirmed his word by the signs that accompanied it" (16:20). Some of us have been to Pemba, Mozambique, and have personally witnessed the lame walking, the blind seeing, and the deaf-mute speaking.

Iris Global Ministry is now active in fifteen nations, with a network of churches that exceeds 10,000. They operate five Bible schools, both for African pastors and for international students, in addition to their three primary schools and school of missions in Pemba.

During mid-2014, thousands of rockets were launched into Israel from Gaza, from the very land Israel had forfeited in an attempt to make peace with their neighbors. Some of us visited Israel during those days and found strong believers who were not holed up in bunkers through the days and nights, but were using the opportunity to take food and supplies to those who were not able to leave their homes. They were light in the darkness, and found people even more open to the gospel of Jesus during the attacks.

A similar thing was happening in Northern Iraq. Believers were using their church buildings and their homes to house refugees. A small group of young Israelis left the greater comfort of their own homes in the Jerusalem area, made their way through Turkey into Northern Iraq in order to deliver aid to the suffering.

> The Calebs and Joshuas of our generation are not afraid of the future.

Believers who are listening to Holy Spirit, the Calebs and Joshuas of our generation, are not afraid of the future. We know the storms are coming, but we are walking with the One who controls the storms and who can keep us safe even in the dangers.

***

The voices of the ten spies say, "Be careful! Protect yourself! Don't take chances!"

The voices of Caleb and Joshua say, "Don't be afraid. Put your trust in the Lord. Walk in His power, His strength. You were brought to the kingdom for these days. Yield your life as a holy instrument that ministers in His strength."

"Even in darkness light dawns for the upright, for the gracious and compassionate and righteous man," the psalmist assures us (112:4).

"Darkness covers the earth and thick darkness is over the peoples, but the LORD rises upon you and his glory appears over you," Isaiah affirms (60:1, 2).

"Under his wings you will find refuge; his faithfulness will be your shield and rampart. You will not fear the terror of night, nor the arrow that flies by day, nor the pestilence that stalks in the darkness, nor the plague that destroys at midday. A thousand may fall at your side, ten thousand at your right hand, but it will not come near you" (Ps. 91:4–7).

"Do not be anxious about anything, but in everything, by prayer and petition, with thanksgiving, present your requests to God," Paul cries out from a Roman jail. "And the peace of God, which transcends all understanding, will guard your hearts and your minds in Christ Jesus" (Phil. 4:6, 7).

These are not simply nice words for church liturgy. They are life! The enemy does not have authority to take our lives prematurely, as long as we walk under the covering of the King.

THE PRESENCE

I have just reread the biography of Bilquis Sheikh[3], a high-born Pakistani woman who became a believer in Jesus and risked her life and everything she held dear in order to express her faith in Jesus through baptism. Bilquis had read Psalm 91, and she walked in an amazing sense of the Lord's Presence. She knew that Muslims who came to faith in Jesus were generally killed for defaming the family honor. Her house was not well protected from intruders, and most of her servants had left their posts out of fear of reprisals for even working for her.

Bilquis's Christian friends began to urge her to put heavy metal grilles over her doors and windows. She reluctantly agreed to the idea and started for the phone to call a repairman, only to realize that "the Presence" had lifted.

She paused, pondered, prayed...and remembered.

Not only did she then refuse to have the doors and windows barred, but she dismissed her servants to their own quarters at nightfall each evening, entrusting herself to the Lord whom she was following. She had read Psalm 91, and she believed it.

A few mornings ago, I awoke with a message emblazoned on my heart, a message I sent to some of those with whom I walk most closely.

"We do not want simply to make it Home ourselves," I told them. "We want to take millions with us." I saw a picture of a gigantic storm, but we were walking *into* the storm, not *away* from it. We were walking forward to rescue those who were perishing.

Another message flashed across my screen: "When the storms come, don't head for the bunker with your food and your guns to hide from the approaching disasters. Move into the storms, assured of His Divine Protection as long as you are in His will."

Learn to distinguish between the voices.

The voices of the ten spies remind us only of the problems. The voices of Caleb and Joshua acknowledge the seriousness of the battle, but point us to the victory. Let us not only be careful to listen to the Calebs and Joshuas of our day, let us *become* those Calebs and Joshuas!

"We should go up and take possession of the land, for we can certainly do it....Do not be afraid... the Lord is with us." We promised to remind you. The LORD is with us, so there is no need for fear. He will work out everything for our good!

NOTES

1. Much more is recorded about this amazing revival in Brother Yun and Paul Hattaway's book, *The Heavenly Man: The Remarkable True Story of Chinese Christian Brother Yun* (Mill Hill, London & Grand Rapids, Michigan: Monarch Books, 2002).
2. https://www.irisglobal.org/about/history
3. Bilquis Sheikh and Richard H. Schneider, *The Miraculous Story of a Muslim Woman's Encounter with God* (Grand Rapids, MI: Baker Book House Company, 1978, 2nd printing, 2003).

CHAPTER 2

EXPECT HARVEST!

Let both grow together until the harvest.
~Matthew 13:30

Our world is not a safe place. Multiple millions have been killed during the wars, persecutions, religious purging, and imprisonments of the 20th and 21st centuries.

Joseph Stalin's reign was responsible for an estimated twenty million deaths of those who would not allow the Soviet leader to become their god.

Adolf Hitler and his National Socialist loyalists are credited with another twelve million, six million of them Jewish people who were murdered in the gas ovens of Auschwitz, Birkenau, and other horrifying death machines.[1]

Communist China is thought to have killed upward of fifty million between 1949 and 1969, with millions more, especially among Christians who refused to abide by the limits of the state-approved form of Christianity, being imprisoned and tortured. When a small group of us smuggled Bibles into China in October of 1989, only a few months following the brutal attack of the student uprising, bloodstains were still visible on the pavement of Tiananmen Square in Beijing.

One and a half million died in Ethiopia after Christian Emperor Haile Selassie was killed and the Communist ruler Mengistu Haile Mariam came to power.

The ruthless henchman, Idi Amin, left Uganda bankrupt, with hundreds of thousands dead and many more having fled their homes during his evil reign in the '70s.

Many North Korean believers have lost their lives during the tyrannical rule of communistic leaders in their land. The March 22, 2014 edition of *World* magazine devoted eight pages to a story chronicling the torture, abuse, imprisonment, and deaths of thousands of North Koreans who dare to believe and to express their belief in Jesus. Thousands of others still live under the daily threat of persecution, as do those who have come to faith in much of the Middle East, Indonesia, and other nations who have no freedom of religious expression.

Taliban, Hezbollah, Hamas, al Qaeda, Muslim Brotherhood, and ISIS spread fear throughout the world. The hope for an Arab Spring has become a nightmare of greater violence.

"Islamic hard-liners stormed a mosque in suburban Cairo, turning it into a torture chamber for Christians who had been demonstrating against the ruling Muslim Brotherhood in the latest case of violent persecution that experts fear will only get worse,"[2] was the news from Egypt in March 2013. Coptic Christians face the daily threats of rape, torture, and intimidation. "Accept radical Islam or be killed,"[3] they are warned. In 2014, world media was filled not only with the reports of publicly televised beheadings of "infidels" from the west, but with the reports of children murdered before their parents' eyes if they did not accept Islam.

After the overthrow of Muammar Gaddafi in Libya, Christians in Benghazi continue to be jailed, tortured, or killed for sharing their faith. "Libyan Christians are being treated similarly to blacks, who since the rebel uprising have been rounded up in their thousands, detained and tortured to death in prison camps merely on the accusation that they worked for Gaddafi, in a barbarous act of ethnic cleansing."[4]

Sister Agnes Mariam, the founder of a monastery in Qara, Syria, has lived in that country since 1994. Some of us were privileged to visit with Sister Agnes in a meeting in Turkey in 2006. In a recent interview on Allen Jones's "Prison Planet," she spoke openly of the disappointment among believers who had assumed that life after Bashir Assad would be better, only to find that Christians have suffered even more intense persecution under the West-backed rebels. An estimated 80,000 believers have lost their lives in recent years.

In October of 1991, I flew with a couple of my friends to Kano, Nigeria, to join Reinhard Bonnke in one of his evangelistic campaigns. We circled the airfield for some minutes before we were given clearance for landing. Then we were whisked away to a secure location because of radical Muslim uprisings that ultimately caused the cancellation of the meetings. For the entire three days of our brief visit, we were in a secluded hideout under police protection. In the dark of night, we were taken to the airport, which remained closed until all of us could be evacuated. We later learned that over two hundred of those who were preparing for the evangelistic meetings had been killed, and that the angry mob was on its way to our hideout as we were being escorted to the airport.

Since the advent of the homicide bombers, no place in the world is secure. This became painfully evident to Americans in the attacks of September 11, 2001.

ATTACK ON AMERICA!

When the planes began their assaults on the Twin Towers, I was at Abraham's Well near Beersheba in Israel. As the report of the first plane striking the World Trade Center was relayed to us, some of our small group wondered if this could possibly be simply pilot error. Nothing like this had ever occurred in the United States. By the time of the second attack, there was no longer any doubt that our nation was under siege.

Our group drove back to Jerusalem, listening intently to additional news of the day's event, and wondering if those in the West would finally understand the daily threats commonplace to Israel, where suicide bombers stalk malls, schools, restaurants, buses, and homes.

Bold headlines in the *Jerusalem Post* the next morning announced: "America under Attack: Thousands die as two hijacked planes destroy World Trade Center." Almost the whole front page of one of the Hebrew language newspapers showed the World Trade Center buildings engulfed in flames. The English headlines read: "We Stand With You, America."

For a day or two following 911, God was welcomed back into the public sector and even into our schools, though in 1962 we had told the Lord to get out of our schools. Prayer was no longer allowed.

GOOD NEWS!

But we have been concentrating on bad news, and bad news demoralizes. Good news energizes. We were not created to be driven by fear, but to live by faith and to have hope.

This is why Paul, writing from a Roman jail, told the believers to "Rejoice!" (Phil. 4:4) and not to be "anxious about anything," that a peace beyond all comprehension would invade our hearts and our minds if we would continue to pray from a point of rejoicing in what God has done, and from a heart full of thanksgiving (see vv. 5–7).

Paul's body may have been in a dungeon, but his heart was full of hope. Why? He lived what he taught. He did not spend time concentrating on the bad news, but on the glorious thought that the good news of Jesus was being spread about, even among the Roman guards (see Phil. 1:13). "Concentrate on things that are true, noble, right, pure, lovely, admirable and excellent," he instructed his fellow travelers (4:8)

> We were not created to be driven by fear, but to live by faith and to have hope.

So I want to be a Caleb, a Joshua and talk about the amazing conquests of God's army that are taking place in the very midst of the horror.

OUR GOD IS GREATER THAN YOUR GOD!

"You come against me with sword and spear and javelin," young David told Goliath, "but I come against you in the name of the LORD Almighty, the God of the armies of Israel, whom you have defied. This day the LORD will hand you over to me" (1 Sam. 17:45–46). Communism, radical Islam or radical Hinduism, and all the other enemies of God may come against us with imprisonments, beatings, and even death, but we will come to them with forgiveness and love and redemption through the Name, the authority, the blood, and the power of Jesus.

Like our predecessors, Caleb and Joshua, we are motivated to go forward in strength. You will not hear good reports from the daily papers or on the evening news. To receive this kind of encouragement, you will need to read material from Youth with a Mission or the Center for World Missions or the Voice of the Martyrs, or hear directly from those who are fighting the battles and experiencing the victories.

The Chinese revival has energized mission intercessors since the first reports of the growing house church movement reached the ears of the Western community of believers. About the same time Israel became a nation, China adopted communist rule. The persecution of believers was so severe that many feared for the survival of any expression of faith in Jesus in that vast nation. Yet, by the time of Israel's Jubilee celebration fifty years later, reports were leaking out that the number of Chinese believers had increased to one hundred seventy million or more. Today the number is still advancing by 30,000 or more a day.[5]

In 2012, Tod was in Kansas City with a group of leaders from the underground church. He was privileged to speak to them and even to challenge them in regard to their *Back to Jerusalem*[6] movement. Not only were they to take the good news of Jesus to the predominantly Muslim nations between China and Israel, but they were to go back to the very nation from which our salvation originated. As Tod began sharing with these Chinese brothers and mentioned the one hundred twenty million believers in China, one of the leaders spoke up with a gentle correction: "One hundred *forty* million!" (Our reports since then have gone as high as one hundred seventy-five million.)

My heart still warms every time I think of the stories from Brother Danyun, who traveled by bicycle through several Chinese provinces to collect stories of the revival.[7]

I will never forget the account of the widowed mother who was arrested and imprisoned for her faith, leaving her three young children at home to be cared for by fellow believers. When she was first incarcerated, she only knew of one other believer among the hundreds of inmates. Eight years later, when she was to be released, over half the prison population and many of the guards had come to faith. As she left the prison gates, she wept over leaving her flock behind.

Among the photos on my iPhone, I still have the picture of Brother Yun, the so-called "heavenly man," whom I met briefly in Jerusalem; later, both Tod and I met him in Nashville. His legs had been intentionally broken so that he would have no hope of escape. But God had a different plan.

Brother Yun experienced a Peter-type deliverance when the Lord told him to get up on his broken legs and walk out of the prison.[8] He obeyed, walking out of his cell through three prison gates that were opened, past guards whose eyes were blinded to his escape, only to find that there was a taxi waiting at the prison entrance. From there, he was taken to a friend's house, from which he escaped to the West. Also like Peter, not until he was outside the prison walls was he sure he was not living in a dream or a vision.

I will also always remember Brother Yun's confession that it is often harder to live radically for the Lord in the Western world than in the detention and concentration camps of China. It is so easy in our soft culture to be lulled into complacent lives of comfort and compromise.

Though in some areas of China, there is today less persecution, other reports as recent as July 29, 2014, speak of an increase of harassment, oppression, and persecution in other sections of the nation.[9]

TEN MILLION BIBLES—IN IRAN!

The Chinese revival is not the only astonishing surprise from the persecuted church. I first found out about the revival in Iran through the September/October 2008 edition of *Mission Frontiers*, a magazine that serves the Center for World Missions.[10] The article began by giving a consensus of Iran's national cabinet concerning the growing Christ-ward movement spreading through the nation: "The only way were (sic) going to stop them is to kill them."

The modern revival began in the early 1960s when a team of American missionaries began to devote themselves to the Persian-Armenian community in Tehran. One of their first disciples was a man named Haik Hovsepian, who was later assassinated for his faith. By the time of his death in 1994, the movement was out of control. There was great unrest, especially among young people. These young people were searching for truth and were convinced that the truth was not to be found in government control. When the government began confiscating Bibles, many of the young people became determined to possess one for themselves. It was estimated, at the time of the writing, that ten million Bibles would not supply the demand. One believer reported that she had personally distributed 20,000 Bibles and had never had anyone turn down her offer.

Christian satellite TV programs became popular and were viewed through satellite dishes that had been illegally smuggled into Iran by the very government officials who had outlawed them. It was estimated that 70 percent of the country was now watching Christian television, and that by the time the article was written, the number of believers had reached a million or more. Some of those Iranian believers with whom I have personally spoken, estimate that revival has now reached seven million or more.

JEW-HATING MUSLIM FINDS TRUE PATH OF PEACE

One young man with whom I visited on Skype had come to Ukraine because he had no hope of studying medicine in Iran. Though he had been raised as a devout Muslim and a radical hater of Jewish people, when he moved to Kiev, for some reason that he himself could not fully explain, he began attending a large Messianic congregation led by Boris Grisenko. He became a serious God-seeker.

One morning at the conclusion of the assembly, my friend saw an older woman sitting behind him, praying. The Lord nudged him: *Go ask her to pray for you.* He cautiously approached the woman with his request.

The lady began to weep. "The Lord told me that a young Muslim man would approach me this morning and ask for prayer," she told him.

My formerly angry, Jew-hating friend had a transformation of heart that morning, a transformation that set him on a path of peace. My own relationship with him came when he showed an interest in translating my *Your People Shall Be My People* book into Farsi (later into Arabic as well). We placed the book on Internet, to be downloaded without cost, so that any Farsi-speaking Iranians, either in their homeland or scattered abroad, would have free access to a book that shows the connection between Israel's salvation and the redemption of the nations.

Another of my Farsi-speaking Iranian friends was reared in a very devout Muslim family in Iran. His mother died when he was four years old, and he became sorely depressed for the next years of his life, a depression that also expressed itself in stuttering so badly that he could not carry on a normal conversation.

By the age of twelve, after a number of other deaths in the family and no forthcoming answers to his constant barrage of questions about God, about death, and about life after death, his father enrolled him in the finest Muslim academy in the city.

"Teach this young man about Allah," the father instructed. "Help him memorize the Koran."

So Amim began memorizing the Koran and learning about Allah. But there was still a great void in Amim's heart. He began to go to the library and search for books about other faiths—Hinduism, Buddhism, or other religions—but nothing seemed to remove the weight inside his heart. One day he asked the librarian if she had a Bible. A secret believer in Jesus, she smiled kindly, but told him, "No, we do not have a Bible." She later found one and gave it to him.

Amim began reading his Bible immediately. He was captivated by the story of the real God who loved His people, but also punished disobedience. Soon he came to the story of Jesus, and, much to his astonishment, without even knowing when it occurred, he realized that the weight in his heart had lifted and that he could carry on a conversation without stuttering. Almost involuntarily, he had begun to believe that Jesus is God's answer and, therefore, had no difficulty surrendering his life to Him.

The love of Jesus will always conquer hatred. Paul said, "Christ's love compels us" (2 Cor. 5:14). "Love your enemies, do good to those who hate you" was Jesus' own admonition (Luke 6:27).

A JIHADIST WHO FOUND JESUS

One of the most difficult places for this love to penetrate may be among the Palestinian terrorists. They have been reared with such intense hatred toward the Jewish people and toward Christians that they would appear impossible to reach. Not so. There are now a number of former terrorists who are bringing their message of love and hope to the world.

One of them is Tass Saada, whose story is told in the book *Once an Arafat Man*.[11] Tass was born in Gaza and raised in Saudi Arabia, in a world of radical Islam and violent Palestinian nationalism. During his teen years, he became a personal friend to Yasser Arafat. By his own admission, he was a killer. He murdered Jews, whether civilians or soldiers. He attacked Christians, sometimes tossing hand grenades into their homes, at other times, strafing them with machine-gun bullets.

In the Foreword to Tass's book, Joel Rosenberg calls him a "jihadist who found Jesus, a violent revolutionary who was radically transformed one day by the power of the Holy Spirit and became a man of peace and compassion," then declares, "This is the story of the greatness of our great God. It is the story of a man who fell in love with a Savior who loves Arabs as well as Jews." [12]

> Most remarkable things happen when we meet Jesus.

Most remarkable things happen when we meet Jesus. Joel spoke of the day he and Tass met. "Here we were, a former aide to PLO Chairman Yasser Arafat and a former aide to Prime Minister Benjamin Netanyahu, hugging each other – not trying to kill each other – in the heart of Jerusalem. All because of the work Jesus had done to give us hearts of love rather than hatred."

I witnessed a similar encounter of another Tass and another Joel one day while visiting Gateways Beyond training school in Cyprus. The room was packed with worshippers, both Jewish and from the nations. I was standing close to the back when a young Arab walked into the room and over to David Rudolph, the leader of the school.

"Is that an Israeli over there?" the young man asked.

"Yes," was David's response.

"I need to wash his feet."

And so, before the entire room full of 75 or 80 of us from the nations, Samer, a former Palestinian terrorist from Lebanon, walked over to Heskel, an officer in the Israel Defense Force, and washed his feet. I cannot read stories like those from Tass and Samer without a smile on my face.

Yes, this is the age when wickedness is increasing, but it is also the age in which righteousness is conquering wickedness. This is a day to be encouraged, not to be dismayed. This is a time when we must remember that all things, yes, *all*, work for our good if we will keep loving the Lord and stay in the calling.

NOTES

1. Many of these statistics and their sources come from Piero Scaruffi, www.scaruffi.com.
2. Paul Joseph Watson, PrisonPlanet.com, March 27, 2013.
3. Ibid.
4. Ibid.
5. This, according to the personal report in a conversation with some of China's key leaders is the movement.
6. http://us.mg204.mail.yahoo.com/dc/launch?.partner=sbc&.gx=0&. rand=fpqm4plsf2pfi - _ftnref6
7. Danyun, *Lilies Amongst Thorns* (Kent, England: Sovereign World Ltd., 1991).
8. Read Acts 12:1–19 to find the very similar deliverance from prison that Peter experienced.
9. See Daniel Wiser's article entitled "China Ramping up Persecution of Christians" in the *Washington Free Beacon*.
10. Krikor Markarian, "Today's Iranian Revolution: How the Mullahs are Leading the Nation to Jesus" www.missionfrontier.com.
11. Tass Saada, *Once an Arafat Man* (Carol Stream, IL: Tyndale House Publishers, Inc., 2008).
12. Ibid., Foreword.

CHAPTER 3

REMEMBER THE PASSOVER

Remember this day.
~Exodus 13:3

I became more acutely aware of the significance of Passover during the Jesus Movement of the late '60s and '70s when Jewish hippies were often becoming "Jesus Freaks" and began to discover the Jewishness of Jesus.

What an intriguing time to be alive! Young people who often had little orientation to anything of God were coming to faith, hungry to know more. Newly-acquired Bibles, wrapped in handmade cloth or leather covers, were in abundance. Parks, storefronts, dorm rooms, flop houses, and street corners served as classrooms. The nearby Little Harpeth River became our large baptismal pool. Swimming pools and bathtubs also worked quite well.

Still on faculty at one of our city's Christian colleges, I would often leave campus, drive to the river with the new believers, dressed in my fashionable knit suit, take off shoes and socks to become the baptizer, then drive back to the campus. By the time I arrived for an afternoon class, only the bottom part of my trousers indicated any unusual activity in which I had been involved!

Many church attendees found the dress of the hippies-turned-Jesus-freaks and a passion for the things of God to be incongruous.

Church business meetings and deacons' groups were faced with a dilemma. Bare feet were not welcomed on plush carpets since business suits and ties were still the appropriate attire for the House of God.

I will never forget one evening in a storefront Bible study I taught when one of our fresh disciples, clad in T-shirt and tattered jeans, rushed toward me, grinning jubilantly. "I read the whole book of Revelation last night!"

I was somewhat stunned since the account of John's apocalyptic visions was, in my estimation, not the best place for a new believer to begin to understand Scripture. Suppressing my judgmental thoughts and trying to keep a straight face, I asked, "What did you learn?"

Exuberantly, my young friend announced, "Evil always loses and good always wins!"

Wow! He got it! I thought, in my best hippie-expressed internal pondering. That really is the message of Revelation! From beginning to end, John urges all future disciples to become passionate followers of Jesus so that they can avoid the plagues and destruction of the future and enter triumphantly into their intended destiny. John serves for us in much the same capacity that Moses and Aaron served Israel during the Passover Exodus: Keep the faith during difficult times; we're getting out of here!

THE ULTIMATE PASSOVER

I call John's apocalyptic visions a depiction of the "ultimate Passover." First, there is a description of how difficult things are among God's people in a foreign land (the letters to the seven churches of Asia). Then the scene changes to describe God's victory Lamb, whose blood releases us from slavery and ushers us into a secure and confident future. As the story unfolds, there are plagues and a Pharaoh-type opponent with his alarming and intimidating team. God's people experience some of the horror, but are ultimately delivered and sing the song of Moses and the Lamb (see Rev. 15:3). I began to understand why these Jewish believers were so fascinated with the apostolic writings. Their own Scriptures were coming alive in Jesus/Yeshua, the Lamb of God, the fulfillment of their prophetic feasts.

The Passover story is the annual day of remembrance that

continually calls Jewish people back to their heritage. "Next year in Jerusalem!" is heralded even among Jewish families who have never been, and never intend to go there. The Passover, even though not always successful in doing so, is a sort of clarion call to Jewish people to remember their roots.[1]

John's Revelation serves much the same purpose. As the seals are opened and the trumpets sound, John calls God's people to repentance. He [John] is the Moses and Aaron, trying to convince Israel not to let the hard times deceive or deter. Victory is ahead.

For hundreds of years, Israel had lived in a land that was not their intended homeland, just as we. Life was hard, as is ours, even in the best of lives. Through all those years of history in Egypt, God's people knew of the promises about their homeland, but the memory held no commanding influence on their humdrum lives - not unlike a great majority of believers, at least in the Western world, where the promises of God have often paled in the face of much activity and the disappointments of daily living.

The message of Revelation, like many of the prophetic words that warn of the future, becomes even more relevant as we see what happened to Israel just before their release. When Moses and his brother Aaron went to the elders of Israel, announcing their soon exodus, and the Israelites "heard that the LORD was concerned about them and had seen their misery, they bowed down and worshiped" (Ex. 4:31). But as that message began to play out in their enslaved lives, rather than rejoicing because the end was near, they became enraged against the very people who were leading them into victory. To make matters worse, the first confrontations between the forces of good and evil did not seem to be overly effective. The magicians of Egypt were able to perform the same miracles that God's representatives produced.

Is this not what Jesus was saying when He told His disciples that in the future, "false Christs and false prophets will appear and perform great signs and miracles to deceive even the elect – if that were possible. See, I have told you ahead of time" (Matt. 24:24–25).

False prophets performing miracles? That's deception! But God has warned us ahead of time. That's mercy!

Notice that Jesus did not say that they would *seem* to perform miracles, but that they will actually be able to perform great miracles.

Not unlike the time of the original Passover, when the magicians of the Pharaoh were able to turn their own rods into snakes (even though Moses' rod swallowed up their rods!), turn water to blood, and cause frogs to be produced. This was *real* power, not just an optical illusion.

In John's picture, the beast out of the sea "performed great and miraculous signs, even causing fire to come down from heaven to earth in full view of men. Because of the signs he was given power to do on behalf of the first beast, he deceived the inhabitants of the earth. He ordered them to set up an image in honor of the beast who was wounded by the sword and yet lived. He was given power to give breath to the image of the first beast, so that it could speak and cause all who refused to worship the image to be killed" (Rev. 13:13–15).

Fire from heaven! Breath to an idol! This from the enemy of God! Dangerous times! No wonder John cries in the middle of his vision, "This calls for patient endurance and faithfulness on the part of the saints....This calls for wisdom!" (13:10, 18).

Do you see why the message of this book is so important for our end-time generation? The enemy will be given great power. We cannot depend only on a demonstration of power. We must become so filled with His Spirit that we are able to discern the source of that power, and can stand with confidence in His presence just as did Stephen (see Acts 7) and other great martyrs of the past.

Even as I write this, I am remembering an older acquaintance of mine whose eyesight had dimmed so that he was almost blind. He had been to medical doctors, and he had asked Christians to pray for him, but nothing had helped. So he was ready to turn to other powers. He learned of an occult leader in the Philippines who had documented cases of healing and was willing to submit to a foreign power in order to gain the victory that he so desperately wanted.

Better to remain blind for a season that to resort to the powers of the enemy that may indeed heal, but will lead us away from the Eternal One!

THE INVINCIBLE ONES

As in the Passover story, John lets us know that only after we have passed through a season of intense adversity/tribulation, will we become the invincible ones. Those who have God's "seal on the foreheads" (Rev. 7:3) are protected from the enemy.

"Fall on us and hide us from the face of him who sits on the throne and from the wrath of the Lamb! For the great day of their wrath has come" (Rev. 6:16–17) is the cry heard in John's Revelation when the seven seals are opened. Though Jesus did not describe seals being opened in heaven, He warns us to expect the kind of conditions John describes in the seals: war, famine, pestilence, natural disasters, and death.

> Those who have God's "seal on the foreheads" are protected from the enemy.

Following the seals, John sees seven angels with seven trumpets. When the trumpets are sounded, the angels release plagues upon the earth: hail, water to blood, and other disasters reminiscent of ancient Israel. John specifically calls these manifestations *plagues*: "The rest of mankind that were not killed by these plagues" (9:20).

That's why the Passover story is so encouraging to me. Israel was in Egypt; we are in our own Egypt. They experienced the hardest season of their lives in Egypt just before the deliverance, just as I believe we will. But then they were spared the last plagues, even though they were still present in Egypt when those plagues were released.

Watch how all this developed:

Plague #1—Water to blood. Israel must have experienced this. There is no mention that they were spared from the same horror that befell all of Egypt.

Plague #2—Frogs. Same thing. An Israelite had to be a strong believer to endure this one without complaining, trusting that God indeed was in the process of delivering them, though they did not understand.

Plague #3—Gnats. Up until this time, the Egyptian magicians were able to produce the same miracles that Moses and Aaron brought forth – water to blood, frogs, but this time, "when the magicians tried to produce gnats by their secret arts, they could not" (Ex. 8:15), and cried out to Pharaoh, "This is the finger of God!" (v. 19).

At this point, things changed for Israel. They were still in the land of Egypt, but they did not experience the plagues of Egypt. Notice how the biblical chronicler records the change:

Plague #4—Flies. "On that day I will deal differently with the land of Goshen, where my people live; no swarms of flies will be there" (Ex. 8:22–23).

Plague #5—Death of livestock. "But the LORD will make a distinction between the livestock of Israel and that of Egypt, so that no animal belonging to the Israelites will die" (9:6).

Plague #6—Boils. "Festering boils will break out on men and animals" (v. 9). Though there is no specific mention this time between Egypt and Israel, the principle has been established and continues with the remaining plagues.

Plague #7—Hail. "The only place it did not hail was the land of Goshen, where the Israelites were" (v. 26).

Plague #8—Locusts. "They will devour what little you have left after the hail…they will fill your houses and those of all your officials and all the Egyptians" (10:5–6).

Plague #9—Darkness. "Total darkness covered all Egypt for three days. No one could see anyone else or leave his place for three days. Yet all the Israelites had light in the places where they lived" (vv. 22–23).

It is important for us to learn from the Exodus and from John's Revelation. The days just prior to Israel's release from four hundred years of slavery and bondage proved to be the most intense time of suffering in all of their history. Not only were they required to produce their quota of bricks for their Egyptian taskmasters, but they had to find their own straw with which to make them (see Ex. 5:6–9).

Not until Israel endured this harshest of all times, the magical power of Egypt's sorcerers, and the horror of the early plagues did they move into a time of protection from the remainder of the plagues.

This message will serve us well as we consider the times of the final Great Tribulation followed by God's wrath being poured out upon the earth.

Plague #10—Death of the firstborn. The last plague was not only a continual judgment upon Egypt and her gods, but was also the foreshadowing of another Lamb who would be slain, and whose blood would be stroked across human hearts for an eternal deliverance from the slavery and bondage that has engulfed Adam's children since that day in the Garden.

Not surprising then that when Jesus' cousin John saw Jesus passing by, he cried out, "Look, the Lamb of God, who takes away the sin of the world!" (John 1:29). Perhaps John was reminded of words from the Torah: "It is the blood that makes atonement for one's life" (Lev. 17:11).

THE BLOOD OF THE LAMB

John the Baptizer knew what he was saying. This Man to whom he was pointing is the fulfillment of every Passover lamb killed through all the centuries. Once His blood was given, there was no longer a need for the slaughter of animals. It seems that God was so intent in getting that message across to the Jewish people and to the whole world that He allowed the Temple in Jerusalem to be destroyed a few years later, after which no further lambs have been sacrificed.

John the apostle picked up on the Passover story as he constantly calls Jesus the Lamb of God who "has freed us from our sins by his blood" (Rev. 1:5). In describing the scene in heaven when the Lamb takes the scroll out of the hand of Him Who sits upon the throne, John hears all of heaven and earth break out in praise:

"You are worthy to take the scroll and to open its seals, because you were slain, and with your blood you purchased men for God from every tribe and language and people and nation" (5:9).

"Worthy is the Lamb who was slain, to receive power and wealth and wisdom and strength and honor and glory and praise… To him who sits on the throne and to the Lamb be praise and honor and glory and power for ever and ever" (vv. 12–13).

Overcomers are victorious because "they have washed their robes and made them white in the blood of the Lamb" (7:14). The "blood of the Lamb" (12:11) secures our victory, and when this Revelation/Passover epic reaches its zenith, the Rider on the white horse is seen descending from heaven with the armies of heaven following, His "robe dipped in blood!" (19:14).

What is the message of the Passover? What is the message from John's Revelation? What is this message that is so relevant for us today? Tough times are coming, but hold on, the best is yet ahead!

NOTES

1. Jewish households for generations have continued the annual celebration of Passover, but this is a remembrance feast for all of us. For those of you who have never observed the feasts, consider the suggestions given in Appendix A for a way to observe Passover, even if you know none of the Jewish liturgy that has come to be associated with this feast.

REJOICE IN SUFFERING!

We also rejoice in our sufferings, because we know that suffering produces perseverance; perseverance, character, and character, hope.
~Romans 5:3–4

Bob and Sandra were one of our "hippie couples" from the days of the Jesus movement. When Sandra became pregnant, she and her husband began to plan for a home birth, which translates: "without anesthesia." Bob received his training as Sandra's coach, and they gathered all the necessary supplies with which to welcome their first child.

When the time arrived and the labor pains began, Sandra was quite excited and even perhaps a bit smug that they had opted for natural childbirth.

But Sandra had never before had this experience. As the pains increased in both frequency and severity, the process was punctuated with vigorous outbursts of alarm. "I'm dying!" she shouted to Bob in dismay. "Do something! Help me!" And when she thought she could bear no more, she screamed, "Don't ever ask me to do this again! I will never have another child!"

As she gasped out those last words, the baby crowned and burst forth into the world. Sandra breathed a huge sigh, looked at her newborn child, then over at Bob. Smiling a bit sheepishly, she confessed, "Oh...I might."

Sandra had experienced what Yeshua described in John 16:21: "A woman giving birth to a child has pain because her time has come; but when her baby is born she forgets the anguish because of her joy that a child is born into the world." The truth Sandra gleaned from her own birthing experience contains the message that is needed for our generation. In fact, that word, *thlipsis* translated "anguish" is the same Greek word often translated "tribulation." When her baby is born she forgets the *thlipsis*/tribulation because of her joy.

> Though we have a secure and magnificent future, the path into that future is not always one of ease.

"We must through much tribulation enter into the kingdom of God" (Acts 14:22 KJV), Paul and Barnabas told the new believers during their first mission journey.

The Roman Jesus-followers were encouraged not only to "rejoice in hope of the glory of God," but to "glory in tribulations also, knowing that tribulation worketh patience, and patience, experience; and experience, hope" (5:2–4 KJV). Or as the New International Version translates: "Rejoice in our sufferings."

Glory in tribulations? Rejoice in suffering? Yes, because, by faith, we see the outcome of our faith.

I call this God's character development plan. "Suffering produces… character" (v. 3 NIV).

GOD'S CHARACTER DEVELOPMENT PLAN

Here in the West, in our attempt to bring more of the unsaved to Jesus, we often do them a disservice by giving them the impression that life will be much easier once they commit their lives to following the Lord. Scripture paints a different picture. Though we have a secure and magnificent future, the path into that future is not always one of ease. Every biblical hero from Genesis to Revelation demonstrates this.

Consider, for example, Joseph, who had all those dreams in his youth. In one dream, the wheat sheaves of his brothers bowed to him in the field. In another, the sun, moon, and eleven stars gave him homage. Nice future, if indeed his dreams were to become reality, but the path to that destiny came with much heartache/persecution/tribulation.

The brothers were enraged with his favorite-son status and his royal, multi-colored robe. The first chance they got, they sold him into slavery to a group of Midianite travelers on their way to Egypt, dipped his coat in animal blood, and pretended he had been killed by a wild beast.

Character formation!

Although he rose quickly in the estimation of his Egyptian master and was put in charge of everything in the master's household, this caused even more trouble. The attractive young man caught the attention of his master's wife, and she tried to lure him into her adulterous arms. Joseph resisted, but her false accusations landed him in prison for over two years.

Perseverance essential!

The prison warden trusted him and gave him authority over the other prisoners. Joseph interpreted dreams for two of his fellow inmates, one of whom promised to remember him when he was restored to his position as cupbearer to the pharaoh, but then promptly forgot all about Joseph.

More character-building!

Joseph passed the test and soon became the most powerful man in Egypt, second only to the king. Only when his brothers made a trip to Egypt to get food during the famine and bowed before him did Joseph "remember his dreams" (Gen. 42:9).

By this time, his character was so well formed that he was able to say to his brothers. "I am your brother Joseph, the one you sold into Egypt! And now, do not be distressed and do not be angry with yourselves for selling me here, because it was to save lives that God sent me ahead of you....So then, it was not you who sent me here, but God" (45:4–8).

All those years, God was weaving His will into Joseph's life, forming him into a person who could govern a nation with wisdom and insight. When the first martyr, Stephen, was reciting the history of Israel, he says that God rescued Joseph "from all his troubles (*thlipsis*—tribulations)" (Acts 7:10), but struck Egypt with famine, "bringing great suffering (*thlipsis*—tribulation)" upon their land (v. 11).

Similar accounts could be given of Abraham, Jacob, Moses, David, Esther, Ruth, and many others who endured immense suffering before entering into their destiny.

Paul's observation of the lives of these former heroes of faith, plus his own life experiences, were the background of those words to the Romans: "Therefore since we have been justified through faith, we have peace...we have gained access...into this grace...And we rejoice in the hope of the glory of God. Not only so, but we also rejoice in our sufferings, because we know that *suffering produces...character!*" (5:1–2, emphasis mine).

Suffering produces character! There is no other way.

DELIGHTING IN DIFFICULTIES

Another biblical scribe admonishes us in this way: "Endure hardship as discipline....No discipline seems pleasant at the time, but painful. Later on, however, it produces a harvest of righteousness and peace for those who have been trained by it....God disciplines us for our good, that we may share in his holiness.... See to it that no one misses the grace of God, and that no bitter root grows up to cause trouble and defile many" (Heb. 12:7, 11, 10, 15).

Suffering produces character! There is no other way

A harvest of righteousness, peace, holiness, and godly character, or a life of bitterness, trouble, and defilement—the choice is ours; the suffering, the "tribulation" will come into every life.

Paul got this message so ingrained within him that he could say to the Corinthians: "I delight in...insults, in hardships, in persecutions, in difficulties" (2 Cor. 12:10).

Delight?

In insults?

Why? Because it afforded him an opportunity to be like Jesus, to forgive, love, and bless.

History is replete with testimonies of persecutors who observed believers during their persecution and who become radical followers of Jesus. Saul of Tarsus is a prime example.

One of our students from the former Soviet Union told how she had been locked in her room and beaten by relatives when she acknowledged her faith in Jesus. Now, years later, almost all of those relatives are followers of the Way they once so despised.

TRIBULATION TRAINING

Corrie ten Boom was the only member of her family to survive the horrors of the Ravensbruck Nazi concentration camp. She saw firsthand that the people of God in Europe were unprepared to go through the difficult times that lay ahead of them during the Nazi reign of terror. The rest of her life was spent imploring people to accept Jesus, but also warning them that perilous times were ahead. "We are in training for the tribulation," she wrote in a letter dated 1974, "but more than sixty percent of the Body of Christ across the world has already entered into the tribulation.

"There are some among us teaching there will be no tribulation, that the Christians will be able to escape all this. These are the false teachers that Jesus was warning us to expect in the latter days. Most of them have little knowledge of what is already going on across the world. I have been in countries where the saints are already suffering terrible persecution.

"In China, the Christians were told, 'Don't worry, before the tribulation comes you will be translated – raptured.' Then came a terrible persecution. Millions of Christians were tortured to death.

"Later I heard a Bishop from China say, sadly, 'We have failed. We should have made the people strong for persecution, rather than telling them Jesus would come first. Tell the people how to be strong in times of persecution, how to stand when the tribulation comes—to stand and not faint.'"[1]

Corrie became so distraught over the effect of the pre-tribulation teaching that she saw it as one of the things against which Jesus warned, a false teaching that would deceive many. In her letter, she stated that these teachers "have little knowledge of what is already going on across the world. I feel I have a divine mandate to go and tell the people of this world that it is possible to be strong in the Lord Jesus Christ."[2]

I, too, have become convinced that the pre-tribulation teaching— that we believers will be caught up into heaven before the last great wave of persecution and tribulation—is a very dangerous teaching. Although it might seem to be an encouragement to people, it can actually serve as deceit. This teaching would be meaningless to today's persecuted church who are suffering imprisonment, torture, and death because of their faith. It would certainly not have been the proper message to send those new believers in Baghdad a few weeks ago.

TRIALS, TROUBLES, AND TRIBULATION

As I pondered all of this, I began to do a very simple Scripture study. I recommend this for everyone. I looked up the Greek word *thlipsis* that is translated "tribulation" in our English Bibles. Interestingly, I found the word rendered by a variety of English words: "affliction(s), afflicted, anguish, burdened, persecution, persecuted, trouble(s), troubled, hardship, sufferings, distress, hard-pressed, harassed, trial(s)."

> The outcome lies not in the magnitude of the storm, but in the quality of the house's foundation.

I began to read through the apostolic writings, using the word *tribulation* every time the Greek word *thlipsis* appears. I found Jesus and the apostles talking about the normal "tribulation" of life, times of "great tribulation" for believers through the centuries, as well as the final "Great Tribulation" that will engulf the whole world shortly before Jesus' return.

In not a single instance do Jesus or the apostles assure us that we would be spared *thlipsis/tribulation*. On the contrary, Scripture after Scripture warn us to be prepared for tribulation, for great tribulation, and even for The Great Tribulation.

In Jesus' parable of the sower and the soils in Matthew 13:3–9 and 18–23 and its parallel passage in Mark 4:3–8 and 13–20, He describes seed (the Word) that fell on hard ground, springs up immediately, but "when [*thlipsis*/tribulation] or persecution comes because of the word, he [the believer] quickly falls away." This is normal "tribulation" that every believer experiences. Jesus warned us to build our spiritual houses upon solid rock, not upon sand. The same storms batter both houses. The outcome lies not in the magnitude of the storm, but in the quality of the house's foundation (see Matt. 7:24–27).

In one of Jesus' last recorded conversations, He answered questions about the time of the end. Reaching back into words from the prophet Daniel, Jesus responded, "For then there shall be *great tribulation (thlipsis)*, such as was not since the beginning of the world to this time, no, nor ever shall be" (Matt. 24:21 KJV; see also Dan. 12:1). Or, in another translation: "There will be great distress (*thlipsis*), unequaled from the beginning of the world until now—and never to be equaled again" (NIV).

This is the final "Great Tribulation," the "Great Distress!"

"*Immediately after the tribulation of those days*...they shall see the Son of man coming in the clouds of heaven with power and great glory. And he shall send his angels with a great sound of a trumpet, and *they shall gather together his elect from the four winds*, from one end of heaven to the other" (Matt. 25:29–31 KJV, emphasis mine; see also Mark 13:24).

Immediately after! This is very clear language. We do not get out before tribulation, before great tribulation, and if we are still around when He is about to return, not before The Great Tribulation. In the apostle John's Revelation, he sees a host of white-robed people from every nation, tribe, people, and language surrounding the throne of God. "Who are they?" John asked one of the elders, and is told, "These are they who have *come out of* The Great Tribulation" (7:14, emphasis mine).

"Have come out of The Great Tribulation!" Very specific! These Godly people have been in The Great Tribulation, and are "coming out!" Jesus seems to have anticipated the theology that would permeate our generation and wanted to make it clear that we have no assurance that we will be spared great trials, not even the last great one.

Forty-three times New Covenant Scripture speaks of "tribulation" (*thlipsis*), always with the exhortation to stand strong, even to the point of persecution or martyrdom.[3] For each eventuality, the admonition is the same: "Prepare!"

THEY ENDURED TO THE END

Because of his radical faith, Richard Wurmbrand spent fourteen years imprisoned in communist Romania—great tribulation. He tells some amazing stories about the strength of those who suffered and often died because of their faith.

A pastor by the name of Florescu was imprisoned and tortured mercilessly. His communist captors used every imaginable cruelty in their attempt to compel him to betray his fellow believers, but he resisted continually. Finally, they brought before him his fourteen-year-old son and began to whip the boy in front of him, assuring the man that they would continue until he gave them the information they sought. When the father could stand it no longer, he cried: "Alexander, I must say what they want! I can't bear your beating anymore!"

"Father," the son replied, "don't do me the injustice of having a traitor as a parent. Withstand! If they kill me, I will die with Jesus on my lips." The torturers continued their assault on the boy until he lay lifeless at their feet. He died, praising God.[4] Though this was not "The Great Tribulation," it was *great tribulation*!

Wurmbrand tells another story of a Christian who was sentenced to death, but was allowed to see his wife one last time. "You must know that I die loving those who kill me," he told his wife. "They don't know what they do, and my final request of you is to love them, too. Don't hold bitterness in your heart because they kill your beloved one. We will meet in heaven." These words penetrated the heart of the officer in charge of the execution.

Years later, Wurmbrand met this former officer, who was imprisoned for accepting the faith for which the earlier brother had been killed. Like Saul of Tarsus, who attended the execution of Stephen (Acts 7), the love of God was more powerful than the weapons of death.[5] This is a story of *great tribulation* followed by *great joy*!

At times there are amazing stories that come from the persecuted church. On one occasion, a young Russian army officer came to a Christian minister in Hungary and asked to see him alone. The minister led him to a small conference room and closed the door. On the wall of the conference room hung a cross.

The brash young officer pointed to the cross and arrogantly said to the minister, "You know that thing is a lie. It's just a piece of trickery you ministers use to delude the poor people to make it easier for the rich to keep them under control."

"But, my poor young man, of course, I believe it," the minister responded, smiling. "It is true."

"I won't have you play these tricks on me!" cried the young man as he drew his revolver and held it close to the body of the minister. "This is serious. Don't laugh at me! Unless you admit to me that it is a lie, I'll fire!"

"I cannot admit that, for it is not true. Our Lord is really and truly the Son of God," said the minister.

The young army officer flung his revolver on the floor and embraced the man of God, tears welling in his eyes. "Then it *is* true!" he cried. "It *is* true! I believe so, too, but I could not be sure men would die for this belief until I found it out for myself. Oh, thank you! You have strengthened my faith. Now I can die for Christ. You have shown me how."[6]

This, too, was great tribulation accompanied by amazing joy.

As in former generations, some of God's saints live miraculous lives while experiencing great anguish. In the words of the writer of Hebrews, they have "through faith conquered kingdoms, administered justice, and gained what was promised…shut the mouths of lions, quenched the fury of the flames, and escaped the edge of the sword. [Their] weakness was turned to strength. [They] became powerful in battle and routed foreign armies. Women received back their dead, raised to life again" (11:33–35a).

Still others, for reasons known only to God, have been "tortured and refused to be released, so that they might gain a better resurrection. Some faced jeers and flogging, while still others were chained and put in prison, They were stoned…sawed in two…put to death by the sword… destitute, persecuted and mistreated—the world was not worthy of them. They wandered in deserts and mountains, and in caves and holes in the ground" (vv. 35b–38).

A part of me does not look forward to this whole process. Like Sandra in the birthing room, we do not enjoy the prospect of hard times or the intensity of the suffering that may lie ahead. Another part of me wants to get it over with so that we can enter into that excellent God-predicted future. Just as surely as the joy of receiving a newborn baby helps a young mother forget the anguish of childbirth, the joy of the future will overshadow whatever suffering we are called upon to endure.

I want to shine! I want to lead many to righteousness. I am assured that everything will be turned for my good if I will stand strong in Jesus. And I am comforted to know that the time of suffering will be short.

NOTES

1. David Pawson, *When Jesus Returns* (London: Hodder & Stoughton Publishers, 2003), p. 199.
2. Ibid.
3. Refer to Appendix B for a complete listing of every New Covenant Scripture that contains the Greek word *thlipsis*, sometimes translated "tribulation," but often translated with other words such as "hardship," "trouble," "distress," "persecution," or "anguish."
4. Richard Wurmbrand, *Tortured for Christ* (Bartlesville, OK: Living Sacrifice Book Company, 1993. Originally published by The Voice of the Martyrs, Inc,, formerly called Christian Missions to the Communist World, Inc., 1967), p. 36.
5. Ibid., p. 45.
6. Ibid., p. 101.

CHAPTER 5

ESCAPE WRATH!

Since we have now been justified by his blood, how much more shall we be saved from God's wrath through him!
~Romans 5:9

I suspect that the strongest motivation of my childhood conversion to Jesus was to escape hell. The fires of hell were well described by roving evangelists. Heaven was not particularly appealing because, at that time, I'd never seen a harp or an angel, and floating on clouds for eternity did little to captivate my childhood imagination.

God never seemed all that upset with my early reason for turning to Him. In fact, Jesus often used this motivation Himself to encourage change. The first words out of the mouth of His predecessor, John, had to do with God's wrath. When John saw the corrupt leadership of his day coming out to hear him preach, he exclaimed, "Who warned you to flee from the coming wrath?" (Matt. 3:7)

There *is* a "coming wrath" of God that will encircle the globe. Jesus Himself, in that discourse with Nicodemus, informs that He came not to pour out God's wrath, but to redeem us *from* that wrath (see John 3:17). "Whoever believes in the Son has eternal life, but whoever rejects the Son will not see life, for God's wrath remains on them" (v. 36).

Those who do not come under God's protection remain under God's wrath. This is a very important distinction. Because of Adam's sin in the Garden and because of our own sins, our world moved out from under God's protection where there is only wrath.

"The wrath of God is being revealed from heaven against all the godlessness and wickedness of men who suppress the truth by their wickedness," Paul wrote (Rom. 1:18). We are "by nature objects of wrath" (Eph. 2:3). "God's wrath comes on those who are disobedient" (5:6), but "Jesus…rescues us from the coming wrath" (1 Thess. 1:10).

A few years ago, I was asked to speak at a prophetic conference. I was aware that most, if not all, those planning the conference ascribed to the "pre-tribulation rapture" theory – that believers will be taken to heaven before the time of The Great Tribulation and most assuredly before the earth experiences God's wrath.

A few days before the conference, one of the planners called. "Are you 'pre-trib'?" I was asked.

"No, I'm not," I replied.

"Pre-wrath?"

"Without question, we never experience God's wrath," I said.

"Okay, that's fine. See you at the conference."

During the meetings, I wanted to be sure to hear some of the speakers who espoused the pre-tribulation theory. I wanted to know where they found Scriptures to support their belief. One of them, a well-known teacher of prophecy, began his message by expressing his belief in this theory, then said, "Now if this is true, then…" and proceeded to bring his entire message based upon his presupposition. He offered no Scriptural documentation, but assumed that everyone believed that we would escape The Great Tribulation.

I sat there, wondering how his message might have changed had he begun with different assumptions, and was left still wondering what Scriptures he had read that made him so confident that we will escape the hard times, the tribulations, even The Great Tribulation.

If I am wrong about all this, and Jesus does, indeed, whisk all of us away before the grand finale of suffering upon the whole world, I will gladly go. But even if for no other reason, I would rather be prepared for the worst and be wrong, than *not* to prepare and be wrong. I have seen too many people walk away from the Lord because He did not live up to their expectation of a carefree life, once they had committed to follow Him.

The ultimate question is whether greater glory comes to God through a lifestyle of surrender that could end even in martyrdom, or whether greater glory comes to Him if we are whisked away before great times of testing. Why would God allow believers all through the centuries to suffer persecution, beatings, imprisonments, and even martyrdom through the vilest of ways, only to release the final generation from being confronted with similar challenges?

Maybe I am a total idealist, but if God will give me the energy and the ability to follow Him passionately, and if I could rescue more for Him by staying behind, and if this would give Him glory, then I would like to be one of His volunteers—even if that means martyrdom.

THE WRATH TO COME

I want to tell you how I came to the conclusion that we are headed for turbulent times, while also walking in assurance that we will escape God's wrath.

Two Greek words—(*orge* and *thumos*)—are translated "wrath" in our Bibles.[1] Both are strong words. One has to do with sudden, violent, passionate outbursts; the other describes an anger that builds up over a long period of time until it finally erupts. Neither is the destiny of a believer.

> Two Greek words are translated "wrath"—Neither is the destiny of a believer....

"God did not appoint us to suffer wrath (*orge*)" (1 Thess. 5:9), Paul assures us. We are "saved from God's wrath (*orge*)" (Rom. 5:9).

When John had all those visions about end times, he saw seals being opened and great distress coming upon the earth, but never in those early chapters did he use the word *wrath* to describe what he saw. Plagues? Yes, but not God's wrath. Only later, when the bowls of wrath are being poured out, does he use that word. Even then he makes it clear that the wrath is not for believers.

"If anyone worships the beast and his image and receives his mark on the forehead or on the hand, he, too, will drink of the wine of God's fury (*thumos*), which has been poured full strength into the cup of his wrath (*orge*)" (Rev. 14:9–10).

At the end of the harvest, the wicked are thrown "into the great winepress of God's wrath (*thumos*)" (v. 19).

THE SEVEN BOWLS

Who experiences God's wrath? Those who have the mark of the beast—the unrepentant. Listen carefully to John's description:

"Another great and marvelous sign: seven angels with seven last plagues—last, because with them God's wrath (*thumos*) is completed" (Rev. 15:1). These seven angels were given the instruction: "Go pour out the seven bowls of wrath (*thumos*) on the earth" (16:1).

As the first bowl was poured on the land, "ugly and painful sores broke out on the people who had the mark of the beast and worshiped his image" (v. 2).

Upon whom? Those who had the mark of the beast. Not on those who have "the seal of God on their foreheads" (Rev. 9:4; see also 7:3, 14:1, and 22:4).

Why would John make this distinction if the believers—those who have the seal of God on their foreheads—are already gone?

Don't forget what happened to Israel! They experienced the first plagues, but then entered into a time of protection even though God's wrath and judgment were being poured out on Egypt. Goshen became Israel's place of refuge—peace in the midst of God's wrath.

In that earlier scene from John's revelation—the woman and the dragon—both she and her seed were taken to a place of protection.

With the emptying of the second bowl, the sea "turned into blood…and every living thing in the sea died" (Rev. 16:3).

The "rivers and springs of water…became blood" (v. 4) when the third bowl was released.

With bowl four, the sun's power intensified, scorching "people with fire. They were seared by the intense heat and they cursed the name of God, who had control over these plagues, but they refused to repent and glorify him" (vv. 8–9).

No repentance! Only cursing!

Bowl number five was aimed directly at the "throne of the beast, and his kingdom was plunged into darkness. Men gnawed their tongues in agony and cursed the God of heaven because of their pains and their sores, but they refused to repent of what they had done" (vv. 10–11).

Judgment is being meted out appropriately to the anti-Christ and his kingdom—those following his evil ways. Still, in spite of intense suffering, there is obstinate rebellion on the part of the lost!

The Euphrates River dried up when the sixth bowl was released "to prepare the way for the kings from the East" so that "the kings of the whole world" could be gathered together "to the place that in Hebrew is called Armageddon...for the battle on the great day of God Almighty" (vv.12–16).

Armageddon, or *Har-Megiddo* (Mountain of Megiddo), is the site of Israel's ancient battleground where decisive battles were won or lost. It appears that this will also be the place where Satan will muster every weapon in his arsenal, hoping against hope that he can somehow regain the victory he temporarily won in the Garden of Eden, but lost in the Garden of Gethsemane. The bowls of wrath apparently serve only to cause Satan and his hosts to dig in their heels even more deeply in their rebellion.

"The seventh angel poured out his bowl into the air, and out of the temple came a loud voice from the throne, saying, 'It is finished!'" (v. 17 NLT).

Believers, protected through the whole process, must breathe a great sigh of relief. The end has arrived.

"Flashes of lightning, rumblings, and peals of thunder" are released in heaven, as the earthquake of all earthquakes strikes the earth. "No earthquake like it has ever occurred since man has been on earth, so tremendous was the quake. The great city split into three parts, and the cities of the nations collapsed....Every island fled away and the mountains could not be found. From the sky huge hailstones of about a hundred pounds each fell upon men. And they cursed God on account of the plague of hail, because the plague was so terrible" (vv. 18–21).

Zechariah also saw a huge earthquake. Same one? This would seem so, since Zechariah's earthquake is also the precursor to the Lord's descent. In neither Zechariah's earthquake nor John's earthquake is the wrath directed toward believers. "This is the plague with which the LORD will strike all the nations that fought against Jerusalem," Zechariah reports.

Great upheavals, but a secure future! The skies are about to open. The earth is being prepared for the return of the King and a reign of peace.

For us? Not to worry. We are secure and protected…even in the hard times, in tribulation.

And during that last great upheaval? We may be here, but we are protected! Just as Israel was in those waning days in Egypt.

He turns everything for our good! Everything!

NOTES

1. See Appendix C for a full description of my study of these Greek words.

WATCH FOR THE SIGNS!

You know how to interpret the appearance of the sky,
but you cannot interpret the signs of the times.
~Matthew 16:3

"How much longer, Daddy? Are we there yet?"

Every parent who has ever been on a long road trip with their children has heard similar questions, and may have answered, "Watch for the signs. They will tell us how far we have to go."

Though the signposts relating to Jesus' return may not be as easy to read as the road signs on an interstate, Jesus assured us that there will be signs that point us to His coming. "You know how to interpret the appearance of the sky, but you cannot interpret the signs of the times," Jesus chided Israel's leaders (Matt. 16:3). "You diligently study the Scriptures because you think that by them you possess eternal life. These are the Scriptures that testify about me" (John 5:39). In other words, "If you were paying attention to your prophets, you would recognize Me."

There are signs that have been in existence for generations. These Jesus calls "the beginning of birth pains"—wars between nations and kingdoms, famines, and earthquakes (see Matt. 24:6–8).

But even these give us hints of the nearness of the Lord. Birth pains start gradually, then increase in both frequency and intensity. Wars, famines, and earthquakes have happened through the centuries, but are proliferating in our day when world peace seems more elusive than ever, and a new kind of war—terrorism and suicide bombing—has invaded the nations.

Among these birth pains there may be hints of space exploration and travel, of eclipses and various other extra-terrestrial manifestations. "There will be signs in the sun, moon and stars" (Luke 21:25). Others see in Jesus' words—"men's hearts failing them" (v. 26 KJV)—a veiled reference to the increase of heart attacks, but that may be a bit contrived. Perhaps all of these have validity and are a part of the birth pains that Jesus described, but in our day the signs seem to be specific fulfillments of prophecy that are, like birth pains, increasing with both frequency and intensity.

ISRAEL BACK IN JERUSALEM

When Jesus spoke of the future of Jerusalem, he predicted that "they (the Jewish people) will fall by the sword and will be taken as prisoners to all the nations. Jerusalem will be trampled on by the Gentiles until the times of the Gentiles are fulfilled....When these things begin to take place...your redemption is drawing near....This generation will not pass away until all these things have happened" (Luke 21:20–32).

"Prisoners to all the nations"—an amazingly apt description of the plight of the Jewish people for all the centuries since the fall of Jerusalem in AD 70.

"Trampled on by the Gentiles"—the Romans, Byzantines, Muslims, Crusaders, Turks, British.

"Until"—Not until 1967 did a sovereign nation of Israel gain possession again of their capital city.

"When these things begin to take place...your redemption is drawing near" (v. 28). These things have clearly begun.

"This generation will not pass away until all these things have happened." Does this mean that the generation who saw Israel's return to Jerusalem will not die before the end of the age and the return of Jesus? It would seem so.

Am I absolutely certain of what I have just written? No. Perhaps I am missing something, but I will let you read the Scripture for yourself and see where your faith lands. I do know that we are to be alert to His coming. Paul tells his Thessalonian brothers and sisters that He is not coming to believers like a thief in the night. In other words, we will be expecting Him. Only to unbelievers does He make a surprise return (see 1 Thess. 5:1–4).

What about Jesus' warning that no one knows about His coming, not even He Himself?

Read His words carefully: "No one knows about that day or hour, not even the angels in heaven, nor the Son, but only the Father" (Matt. 24:36).

Not the day nor the hour, but Jesus, in the same setting, indicates that we will know the season. His coming would be "as it was in the days of Noah" (v. 37).

How was it in the days of Noah? Unbelievers were completely caught off guard, but Noah knew the season. The ark was prepared and the animals began to come.

JEWISH PEOPLE ARE COMING TO FAITH

During that last week of Jesus' life, when He knew that He would soon be executed, He began to give other clues about His return.

"O Jerusalem, Jerusalem!" He wept as He looked back one day on His way up the Mount of Olives. "Your house is left to you desolate. For I tell you, you will not see me again until you say, 'Blessed is he who comes in the name of the Lord'" (23:37–39).

Clue #1: Jesus will not return until a significant number of Jewish people, even Jewish leaders, are ready to receive Him. "The Temple will be destroyed, but you will again return to Jerusalem and will be ready to welcome Me before I return" (my paraphrase).

Soon after Jerusalem's devastation, the message of the kingdom of God reached throughout the Roman Empire and ultimately all over the world, though few Jewish people came to faith during those centuries, and there was no representation of the body of believers in Jerusalem—no leaders to welcome Jesus back.

With the rise of the reformers of the 16th century, as men and women began to read the Word for themselves, things changed. They grew to expect both Israel's restoration to the Land and the salvation of Israel.

The Geneva Bible, published in 1560, arose out of that believers' movement. Commenting on one of Paul's remarks to the Romans, the Geneva Bible says, "When both they (the Jews) and the Gentiles shall embrace Christ, the world shall be restored to a new life."[1]

In other words, "The Jews will one day turn to Jesus."

William Perkins, professor at Christ's College in Cambridge in 1579, wrote confidently about a time when the Jewish nation would come to know their Redeemer: "I gather that the nation of the Jews shall be called, and converted to the participation of [the blessing given to Abraham]; when, and how, God knows, but that it shall be done before the end of the world we know."[2]

Eighteenth-century Church of Scotland preacher Thomas Boston was confident, along with many of his peers, that a time would come when Israel would be redeemed. In a sermon preached in 1716, on "Encouragement to Pray for the Conversion of the Jews," he said, "There is a day coming in which there shall be a national conversion of the Jews or Israelites. The now blinded and rejected Jews shall at length be converted into the faith of Christ, and join themselves to the Christian Church."[3] We may not like the way Thomas Boston expressed himself; we may not believe that these returning Jewish believers will need to "join themselves to the Christian Church," but rather be gathered in their own synagogues to worship their Messiah Yeshua/Jesus. We may even wince at the use of the word *convert* as though they have left their Jewish faith and joined another religion, when in reality they have simply completed the faith of their childhood by reclaiming their own God, the God of Abraham, Isaac, and Jacob, and the promises of their coming Messiah. But Boston had caught hold of a truth that would only later come to fruition. /

Boston even understood that the salvation of Israel would effect world revival. In referencing Paul's remarks in Romans 11:12 and 15, he wrote, "Are you longing for a revival to the churches, now lying like dry bones, would you fain have the Spirit of life enter into them? Then pray for the Jews. 'For if the casting away of them be the reconciling of the world; what shall the receiving of them be, but life from the dead?'"[4]

This expectation of Israel's coming to faith continued to thrive by the time of Charles Spurgeon in the 19th century. In an 1855 volume of sermons, he wrote, "The day shall come when the Jews...shall be gathered in again. Until that shall be, the fullness of the church's glory can never come."⁵

All these from earlier centuries were seeing in the Spirit what we have seen with our own eyes—Israel's return to the Land and Jewish people coming to the Lord in increasing numbers. Only in recent years have we begun to understand that Jesus was prophesying that a significant number of Jewish people in Jerusalem would be ready to receive Him before His return.

The year 1967 was an amazing year for the beginning of this fulfillment. Not only was this the year Israel took Jerusalem in the Six-Day War, but this was also the beginning of the movement in which tens of thousands of Jewish men and women began to believe that Jesus/Yeshua is indeed the Promised Messiah of Israel.

> The Jesus Movement produced most of today's senior leaders in the Messianic movement.

The lead article in the June 21, 1971 edition of *Time Magazine* is about "The Jesus Revolution." Three times the article mentions the beginning of what also came to be called the "Jesus Movement" and was the beginning of the charismatic movement. Writer Richard Ostling, describing the unusual revival of those former hippies-turned-Jesus freaks, casually mentions: "Many Jews have also joined, claiming that they are not quitting, but fulfilling their Judaism."⁶

Ostling's statement is quite the understatement! The Jesus Movement produced most of today's senior leaders in the Messianic movement. This was the movement that captured my own heart for the things of the Spirit and, because of Jewish people that were coming to faith in my own congregation, launched me into a passion for the Lord from which I have never recovered. Through these Jewish believers, I became acquainted with the burgeoning Jewish believing movement and into a rereading of the Prophets.

Prior to 1967, there were occasional Jewish people who believed in Jesus, but the Jesus Movement was the first revival since the first century that began an avalanche of Jewish people coming to faith. This has resulted in several hundred thousand Jewish believers now scattered in churches, in freshly formed Jesus-believing synagogues or house groups, or simply remaining in a traditional synagogue as believers. One of my reasons for writing *Your People Shall Be My People* was to show the correlation between the Jewish return to the Land and their coming to faith as predicted in Isaiah 6, believing that since the Land is no longer devastated, the time has come for Jewish eyes to be open to their God and their Messiah.

This opening of Jewish eyes continues its advance, though not nearly as rapidly as some of us would desire. The Jewish community is also changing its view of Jewish believers. A 2013 Pew Forum survey of American Jewry, showed that 34 percent of American Jews now agree that a person can still be Jewish even if he believes that Jesus is the Messiah. This would have been impossible a generation ago.[7]

Jesus pointed to all of this when He said that day on the Mount of Olives, "You will not see me again until you say, 'Blessed is He that comes in the Name of the Lord!'" as if to say, "I will not return until you are ready to welcome me."

This could happen at any time.

REVIVAL AMONG THE NATIONS

In Jesus' same conversation that day on the Mount of Olives, in warning of the events that would precede His return, He told His followers, "This gospel of the kingdom will be preached in the whole world as a testimony to all nations (*ethnos*—ethnic group), and then the end will come" (Matt. 24:14).

Clue # 2: "To all nations!" If we understand this accurately, Jesus will only return when every ethnic group of the world has learned of Him, with many following Him. "Every tribe and language and people and nation" (Rev. 5:9; 7:9) must be represented around the throne of God.

Another reason for the *Your People Shall Be My People* book was to connect the present world revival in China, Africa, Indonesia, South America and even the Middle East among the Muslims, to the return of Jewish people to their land. "If their transgression means riches for the world, and their loss means riches for the Gentiles (the nations), how much greater riches will their fullness bring" (Rom. 11:12) were Paul's words to the Romans.

In other words, "Just you wait! When Israel begins to come to know their Messiah, there will be an amazing revival of faith awakened in all the world—greater riches for everyone!"

In the late 20th century, mission agencies around the world caught hold of Jesus' prediction and began a concerted effort to evangelize the unreached people groups of the world. "AD 2000 and Beyond" was formed, targeting those unreached groups. When the task remained unfinished by the turn of the century, other organizations arose.

Table 71 is "a loose association of Christian organizations committed to working together in partnership among the remaining unreached people groups in the world."[8]

The Joshua Project "is a research initiative seeking to highlight the ethnic people groups of the world with the fewest followers of Christ. Accurate, regularly updated ethnic people group information is critical for understanding and completing the Great Commission."[9]

"call2all" is "a worldwide movement, calling the church, leaders, and organizations networking together to finish the Great Commission."[10]

Larry and Connie Lovell are symbolic of hundreds or thousands who have devoted themselves to the fulfillment of Jesus' words. They have spent the majority of their adult lives with the small tribe of less than 15,000 Mineveha people in Ukarumpa, Papua New Guinea, in order to translate the New Testament Scriptures into the Mineveha language and tell them about Jesus. The hundreds of Mineveha believers in Jesus who presently work alongside the Lovells in their translation of the Old Testament writings are the fruit of Larry and Connie's life work.

"This gospel of the kingdom will be preached in the whole world as a testimony to all nations, and then the end will come."

We are drawing close.

NATIONS AGAINST ISRAEL

In Zechariah's description of the conditions just prior to Jesus' coming, he says, "I will gather all the nations to Jerusalem to fight against it....Then the LORD will go out and fight against those nations....On that day his feet will stand on the Mount of Olives" (vv. 3–4).

Clue # 3: All the nations will gather to fight against Jerusalem. "The city will be captured, the houses ransacked, and the women raped" (v. 2). This is not a pleasant depiction of the conditions prior to Jesus' return.

The only way I can read this with any degree of hope is to remember that in those last days of Israel's stay in Egypt, as conditions worsened, those who were obedient to God were protected from the horror.

Clue # 4: The city of Jerusalem will be divided.

"Half of the city will go into exile, but the rest of the people will not be taken from the city" (v. 2). Not God's ultimate plan, but this has been the recommendation of the United Nations for decades. Give half the city to Israel's worst enemies, enemies who have yet to acknowledge Israel's right to exist, and who still consider the nation of Israel to be "occupied territory."

A November 25, 2013, web-based report from UN Watch, states that "The U.N. General Assembly in 2013 adopted a total of 21 resolutions singling out Israel for criticism — and 4 resolutions on the rest of the world combined....The four that do not concern Israel are: one on Syria, a regime that has murdered 120,000 of its own people, and one each on Iran, North Korea and Myanmar. There were zero UNGA resolutions on gross and systematic abuses committed by China, Cuba, Egypt, Pakistan, Russia, Saudi Arabia, Sri Lanka, Sudan, Zimbabwe, nor on many other major perpetrators of grave violations of human rights."[11]

Strangely close to Zechariah's prediction! To perceive the leadership of all the nations turning against the nation of Israel is not difficult to imagine. Zechariah's picture may be near, but I am encouraged to believe that this end-time attack will be of short duration.

"Then the LORD will go out and fight against those nations as he fights in the day of battle. On that day, his feet will stand on the Mount of Olives" (14:3), "the LORD my God will come with all the holy ones with him" (v. 5), the ensuing earthquake will open up the Eastern Gate (see Ezek. 44:1), water will flow out from Jerusalem, down to the Dead Sea (see Ezek. 47), and "the LORD will be king over the whole earth" (v. 9).

These signs could happen very soon, but as we look more carefully at the road signs, we are forced to pause, like pulling over to a roadside park to study the map, and must finally admit that some of the roads on our path are not clearly marked, or at least that we do not have the expertise with which to read them.

Zechariah 12 also has a prediction of war that may or may not be the same war described in Zechariah 14. In the earlier depiction, "all the nations are gathered against" Jerusalem (12:3), but the prophet seems to indicate that Israel will be victorious in that battle.

"I am going to make Jerusalem a cup that sends all the surrounding peoples reeling....I will make Jerusalem an immovable rock for all the nations. All who try to move it will injure themselves....The leaders of Judah will say in their hearts, 'The people of Jerusalem are strong, because the LORD Almighty is their God.' On that day I will make the leaders of Judah like a firepot in a woodpile, like a flaming torch among sheaves. They will consume right and left all the surrounding peoples, but Jerusalem will remain intact in her place....On that day the LORD will shield those who live in Jerusalem, so that the feeblest among them will be like David, and the house of David will be like God, like the Angel of the LORD going before them. On that day I will set out to destroy all the nations that attack Jerusalem" (vv. 2–9).

Israel will see Jesus.

This statement rings of a great national victory, but no mention of the Lord's army visibly entering the battle.

"I will pour out on the house of David and the inhabitants of Jerusalem a spirit of grace and supplication," Zechariah continues. "They will look on me, the one they have pierced, and they will mourn for him as one mourns for an only child, and grieve bitterly for him as one grieves for a firstborn son....On that day a fountain will be opened to the house of David and the inhabitants of Jerusalem, to cleanse them from sin and impurity" (12:10–13:1).

Israel will *see* Jesus. They will grieve when they realize that they had rejected their Messiah, but their grief soon turns to joy as they experience the cleansing from sin and impurity.

Is this a *seeing* with natural eyes, or is this a *vision-seeing of Jesus* much like my friend Eitan Shishkoff had that day in the mountains of New Mexico when he *saw* Jesus on the cross with Jesus' blazing eyes piercing Eitan's soul? We are not likely to know until it happens.

GOG AND MAGOG

Where does Ezekiel 38 and 39 fit into this picture?

"In future years… after many days" (38:8), an invading army is to come against Israel. The enemies are Gog and Magog, nations "from the far north," and include Persia (Iran), Ethiopia and/or Egypt (Cush), Libya (Put), parts of Assyria, and other nations. These nations invade "a land that has recovered from war," who has been brought back to their land after long desolation, but who now "live in safety." (vv. 8–9).

Recovered from war and living in safety? This is not a description of today's Israel. Threats of war abound daily with rockets from Gaza or Lebanon and suicide-bombing terrorists lurking in every city. The war Ezekiel describes, like the one in Zechariah 12, is one in which Israel is remarkably victorious. God intervenes with exacting judgment.

"I will summon a sword against Gog on all my mountains," Ezekiel continues. "I will execute judgment upon him with plague and bloodshed. I will pour down torrents of rain, hailstones and burning sulfur on him and on his troops and on the many nations with him….I will make myself known in the sight of many nations" (vv. 21–23).

The victory is so decisive that "for seven months the house of Israel will be burying [the dead] in order to cleanse the land" (39:12), and for seven years, enemy weapons supply fuel for the nation (see 38:9).

What about John's depiction of Gog and Magog? The Gog Magog battle he describes follows the millennial reign of Jesus. "*When the thousand years are over*, Satan will be released from his prison and will go out to deceive the nations in the four corners of the earth—Gog and Magog—to gather them for battle" (Rev. 20:7–8, emphasis mine). "In number they are like the sand on the seashore. They marched across the breadth of the earth and surrounded the camp of God's people, the city he loves. But fire came down from heaven and devoured them. And the devil, who deceived them, was thrown into the lake of burning sulfur….tormented day and night for ever and ever" (vv. 8–10).

Is John's battle the same as Ezekiel's battle? Is Ezekiel's battle also at the end of the millennium? He, too, spoke of "burning sulfur" being poured on the enemy and his troops.

Using enemy weapons as fuel for the nation does not sound

like my understanding of Jesus' beginning years of the millennial reign of peace with a rebuilt Temple in Jerusalem. Burying the dead for seven months does not have the ring of a joyful celebration of His new government.

Are there two battles that engage Gog and Magog in a double-prophecy fulfillment? Until the prophecies take place, we will not have a clear picture. As Paul told Corinth, "We see but a poor reflection as in a mirror. Then we shall see face to face" (1 Cor. 13:12).

We have many questions, and not always the answers.

> Until the prophecies take place, we will not have a clear picture.

RISE OF THE ANTI-CHRIST

Clue # 5. One thing is certain. An anti-Christ figure will dominate the world stage as we approach the end. In Paul's second letter to the Thessalonians, he tells the believers, "That day (Jesus' return) will not come, until the rebellion occurs and the man of lawlessness is revealed, the man doomed to destruction. He will oppose and will exalt himself over everything that is called God or is worshiped, so that he sets himself up in God's temple, proclaiming himself to be God" (2:3–4).

This is clear language—an anti-Christ in a reconstructed Temple, presenting himself as God.

This anti-Messiah figure is the same man Daniel saw, one "who speaks against the Most High" (7:25), who "will consider himself superior… will take his stand against the Prince of princes" (8:25), and will "exalt and magnify himself above every god and will say unheard of things against the God of gods" (11:36).

This is the beast from the sea in John's Revelation, who "opened his mouth to blaspheme God and to slander his name and his dwelling place and those who live in heaven" (Rev. 13:5–6)— the one who reigns over the earth for 3½ years.

This future world leader will be Satan's personal representative in his final attempt to lead all of Adam's family astray and to prevent the return of King Jesus.

THOSE LAST SEVEN YEARS

Daniel's vision contains a number of predictions about "the time of the end" (12:4, 9, 13), specific prophecies about the coming of "Messiah" (9:25 KJV), and this future world ruler "waging war against the saints and defeating them" (7:21), who will "destroy the city and the sanctuary" (9:26). This evil prince will "confirm a covenant with many for one 'seven.' In the middle of the seven he will…set up an abomination that causes desolation, until the end that is decreed is poured out on him" (v. 27). In the same context, Daniel is told, "The end will come like a flood" (v. 26).

A seven-year covenant with something changing in the middle of the seven years—thus two 3 ½-year time spans.

Daniel describes this "distant future" (8:26) when, during two 3 ½-year time spans, "a stern-faced king, a master of intrigue, will arise" (8:23). "He will become very strong, but not by his own power. He will cause astounding devastation and will succeed in whatever he does. He will destroy the mighty men and the holy people. He will cause deceit to prosper and he will consider himself superior…he will take his stand against the Prince of princes" (vv. 24–25).

Daniel's last seven years seem to include both the 3 ½-year time of The "Great Tribulation," plus the emptying of the bowls of wrath just prior to the end—a time when, if believers are still here, they are shielded from God's wrath.

Daniel's prophecy is very clear about the earlier 3 ½-year prediction when "the saints will be handed over to [the evil ruler] for a time and times and half a time" (7:25). John mentions the same length of time, called "forty-two months," when this world dictator "was given power to make war against the saints and to conquer them" (Rev. 13:4–5).

KEEP ON KEEPING ON!

There are many signs along this road. Some are clear; some are difficult to read. One thing is sure. We are called to lives of right thinking and right actions.

"I have written…to stimulate you to wholesome thinking," Peter admonished when he wrote of the last days (2 Pet. 3:1). "What kind of people ought you to be? You ought to live holy and godly lives as you look forward to the day of God and speed its coming….Make every effort to be found spotless, blameless and at peace with him" (vv. 11–13).

As we observe the signs, two things we must remember: we are victorious through it all, and we are more powerful than any force that can attack us. The darkest days are our brightest hours.

NOTES

1. Iain H. Murray, *The Puritan Hope: Revival and the Interpretation of Prophecy* (Carlisle, PA: The Banner of Truth Trust, 1971, reprinted in 1998). This book is the source of this quotation (see page 72) and a number of other quotations from such notable men of faith as Jonathan Edwards and Charles Spurgeon.
2. Ibid., p. 42.
3. Ibid., p. 46.
4. Ibid., p. 114.
5. Ibid., p. 256.
6. Richard Ostling, "The Jesus Revolution," *Time*, June 21, 1971.
7. Drew Desilver, "Jewish Essentials: For most American Jews, ancestry and culture matter more than religion," October 1, 2013, www.pewresearch.org.
8. This description comes from the Table 71 website: http://wptestweb.wordpress.com
9. Their own description as posted on their website: http://joshuaproject.net/joshua-project.php
10. See this website for a further description of call2all: http://call2all.org
11. "2013 at the UN: 21 resolutions against Israel, 4 on rest of the world," UNWatch, Monitoring the Nations, Promoting Human Rights, Unwatch.org/November 25, 2013.

CHAPTER **7**

DON'T BE DECEIVED!

Watch out that no one deceives you.
~Matthew 24:4

"My feelings as a Christian points me to my Lord and Savior as a fighter…. In boundless love as a Christian and as a man I read through the passage which tells us how the Lord at last rose in His might and seized the scourge to drive out of the Temple the brood of vipers and adders….As a Christian I have no duty to allow myself to be cheated, but I have the duty to be a fighter for truth and justice….For as a Christian I have also a duty to my own people."[1]

These are the words of Adolf Hitler spoken in Munich on April 12, 1922.

"We demand liberty for all religious denominations in the State, so far as they are not a danger to it and do not militate against the morality and moral sense of the German race," Hitler continued. "The Party, as such, stands for positive Christianity, but does not bind itself in the matter of creed to any particular confession."

"Positive Christianity!"

Hitler's deceptive words caught the church off guard. Over 90 percent of the German people were baptized and confirmed "Christians." Thousands of leaders bought in to Hitler's idea of "positive Christianity," a Christianity that expelled Jews and Jewish-believing leaders from the church so that the races could remain pure. In those early days, there was no mention of eradicating the Jews, but simply separating them to themselves.

Eric Metaxas's biography of Dietrich Bonhoeffer described the rationale of those leaders: "Someplace in the deep and wide abyss betwixt these two existed a strange group who did not think there was an abyss, and who wished to create a seamless connection between National Socialism and Christianity. They saw no theological problem with the project, and during much of the 1930s, they constituted a powerful force in Germany.... One German Christian leader, Reinhold Krause, said that Martin Luther had left Germans with 'a priceless legacy: the completion of the German Reformation in the Third Reich.'"[2]

Martin Luther, almost four centuries earlier, had prepared the way for this kind of thinking. Even though, in his early years, he had encouraged gentleness in dealing with the Jewish people, hoping that this would result in their conversion to Christianity, in his later years he became vehemently anti-Semitic. In those closing years of Luther's life, he became so irate by Jewish refusal to accept Christianity that he "proposed seven measures of 'sharp mercy' that German princes could take against the Jews: (1) burn their schools and synagogues; (2) transfer Jews to community settlements; (3) confiscate all Jewish literature, which was blasphemous; (4) prohibit rabbis to teach, on pain of death; (5) deny Jews safe-conduct, so as to prevent the spread of Judaism; (6) appropriate their wealth and use it to support converts and to prevent the lewd practice of usury; (7) assign Jews to manual labor as a form of penance."[3]

Luther's words became fodder in the hands of Hitler and his "positive Christianity" followers.

"Many of [the pastors] honestly believed that under Hitler the opportunities for evangelism would increase, but Bonhoeffer and others knew that a church that did not stand with the Jews was not the church of Jesus Christ, and to evangelize people into a church that was not the church of Jesus Christ was foolishness and heresy."[4]

Nazism could not seduce those who were spiritually astute. In the beginning of Hitler's reign, Bonhoeffer helped to form what came to be known as the "Confessing Church," working against the "Nazified official German Church."[5] Before his martyrdom, he also led an underground seminary, teaching his seminarians "how to maintain a robust devotional life, praying and studying and meditating on the Scripture daily."[6]

LET NO ONE DECEIVE YOU!

"Watch out that you are not deceived," Jesus Himself warned.

"Let no one deceive you with empty words," Paul later admonished (Eph. 5:6).

"I tell you this so that no one may deceive you by fine-sounding arguments" (Col. 2:4).

"Evil men and impostors will go from bad to worse, deceiving and being deceived" (2 Tim. 3:13).

"The Spirit clearly says that in later times some will abandon the faith and follow deceiving spirits and things taught by demons" (1 Tim. 4:1).

Abandon the faith! Deceived by spirits! Taught by demons! Strong warnings!

A few years ago I stood on the platform of the Reichsparteigelände (Nazi Party rally grounds) in Nuremburg, Germany, the platform from which Hitler later empowered his SS troops. Not until then had I known that Hitler's chosen platform was an enlarged replica of the temple in ancient Pergamum, the temple that John described as the place "where Satan has his throne" (Rev. 2:13). There are no coincidences. Someone, perhaps even Hitler himself, knew about Pergamum. There was an invoking of demonic powers from that place. And the rest is history...heart-wrenching history.

The seduction that engulfed the German Church was also working among communist countries of Eastern Europe. "Once the communists came to power, they skillfully used the means of seduction toward the Church," Richard Wurmbrand wrote in his book *Tortured for Christ*.

The communist government convened a gathering of Christian leaders in the Rumanian national parliament building. "There were four thousand priests, pastors, and ministers of all denominations. These four thousand priests and pastors chose Joseph Stalin as honorary president of this congress. At the same time he was president of the World Movement of the Godless and a mass murderer of Christians. One after another, bishops and pastors arose…and declared that communism and Christianity are fundamentally the same and could coexist" assuring "the new government of the loyalty of the church."[7]

One orthodox bishop had the hammer and sickle emblem stitched onto his clerical robes, asking that he now be called "Comrade Bishop." A Lutheran bishop began to teach in the theological seminary that God had given three revelations through Moses, Jesus, and Stalin, each superseding the one before. At times, church pastors became officers in the secret police, working to silence those who had remained true to their faith, often assigning them to years of imprisonment and even death.

> Traditional Christianity will not shield us from deception.

Richard and his wife, Sabina, were in that large gathering. They listened as one minister after another praised Stalin and the communist regime. Sabina turned to her husband and said, "Richard, stand up and wash away the shame from the face of Christ! They are spitting in His face." Richard told her, "If I do so, you lose your husband." Sabina's response? "I don't wish to have a coward as a husband."[8]

Richard and Sabina both spent years in communist prisons because of their unwillingness to compromise their faith.

FROM YOUR OWN NUMBER!

"After I leave, savage wolves will come in among you and will not spare the flock," Paul told the Ephesian elders. "Even from your own number men will arise and distort the truth...so be on your guard!" (Acts 20:29–31).

The power of deception! "From your own number!"

Traditional Christianity will not shield us from deception. Being members of a church will not suffice. Listening to radio and TV evangelists is not enough. Quoting or referencing Scripture may even add to the confusion since the devil himself is quite adept at citing Scripture out of context. Like Jesus, we must be ready to reply, "It is written!" (see Luke 4:1–13).

We must know Jesus. His Word must be in our hearts and in our minds. The Holy Spirit's voice must be our Guide. Those who walk intimately with Jesus will be kept from deception.

THE LAST GREAT DECEIVER

Both Stalin and Hitler were precursors of the coming world deceiver, yet neither of these is credited with the kind of power that will accompany that last great deceiver.

"False Christs and false prophets will appear and perform signs and miracles to deceive the elect—if that were possible" (Mark 13:22). "Watch out that you are not deceived" (Luke 21:8).

Deceit often comes from people who look like "good" church members, fellow Christians, preachers, pastors, teachers, evangelists!

"Satan himself masquerades as an angel of light" (2 Cor. 11:15).

"The coming of the lawless one will be in accordance with the work of Satan displayed in all kinds of counterfeit miracles, signs and wonders, and in every sort of evil that deceives those who are perishing. They perish because they refused to love the truth and so be saved. For this reason God sends them a powerful delusion so that they will believe the lie and so that all will be condemned who have not believed the truth but have delighted in wickedness" (2 Thess. 2:9–12).

"He (the antichrist) performed great and miraculous signs, even causing fire to come down from heaven to earth in full view of men. Because of the signs he was given power to do on behalf of the first beast, he deceived the inhabitants of the earth. He ordered them to set up an image in honor of the beast who was wounded by the sword and yet lived. He was given power to give breath to the image of the first beast, so that it could speak" (Rev. 13:13–15).

Counterfeit miracles, signs, and wonders! Satan as an angel of light! People refusing truth! Powerful delusions sent by God Himself to those who have refused truth!

Strong warnings!

BEWARE OF SMALL COMPROMISES!

The evils of communism and Nazism seem evident to us in retrospect. But deception comes gradually. The compromises seem so easy, even safe in the beginning. Yet they ultimately take us down the slippery slope of destruction.

Often the enemy's trickery comes in very subtle ways, directed toward us as individuals. A small compromise can propel one down a path of disbelief and apostasy.

Years ago, I had an encounter following a Wednesday evening Bible class. A man, probably in his mid-forties, approached me and asked if we could speak privately for a few minutes. We drew aside and he began to tell me about his life. He had lost faith in God, he informed me. He had once been a missionary in a foreign country. While in that country, he had had an affair that changed the course of his life. Although he had earlier experienced the power of the Holy Spirit, he had never taught about that power; his supporting church back home did not agree with his theology, and he knew that he would have lost financial support if he preached his newfound convictions.

As he spoke, I remembered words from Paul to the Colossians, that our actions may often affect our faith. "Once you were alienated from God and were enemies in your minds because of your evil behavior" (1:21).

Alienated because of your evil behavior, I mused.

"When did you have the affair?" I asked my new friend. "Before or after you compromised your convictions regarding the work of the Spirit?"

"After," he replied.

"That's the reason you had the affair," I said. "And when did you lose your faith...before or after the affair?"

"After."

"That explains your loss of faith."

Deception had crept gradually into my friend's life.

Another of my friends says, "Sin always takes us further than we intended to go, we pay more than we intended to pay, and we stay longer than we intended to stay."

BEWARE OF FALSE DOCTRINE!

Some of the Church of the 21st century has already crossed over the threshold of deception. The liberalism of the 18th and 19th centuries began an interpretation of the Resurrection that did not include Jesus' physical body coming out of the tomb:

Maybe the women went to the wrong tomb.

Wrong tomb for the most important figure in your life? Not likely!

Perhaps the disciples stole the body away in order to promote Him as Israel's Messiah.

Disciples stole His body, then gave their lives and suffered persecution for a lie? I don't think so.

One 20th-century theologian proposed the "Passover plot"—that Jesus helped to plan His own appearance of death in order to fake His resurrection and further His teaching.

Passover plot! Sure! Then, after all the beating and apparent death from the cross, to appear three days later in a robust body that still has scars? Impossible!

Maybe the disciples were hallucinating—they so wanted Him to be resurrected that they "saw" Him.

Hallucinating? I love Paul's words to Corinth. "He appeared to more than five hundred of the brothers at the same time, most of whom are still living" (1 Cor. 15:14). Five hundred hallucinating at the same time? In other words, "If you do not believe He arose," Paul seems to be saying, "then send someone back to Jerusalem and find some of those brothers who saw Him bodily. Jesus came out of the grave. These people touched Him, saw Him, ate with Him. These are not the actions of a spirit, but a person who lives."

"If Christ has not been raised, our preaching is useless and so is your faith. More than that, we are then found to be false witnesses about God, for we have testified about God that he raised Christ from the dead. But…if Christ has not been raised, your faith is futile; you are still in your sins" (1 Cor. 15:14–17), Paul furthered elaborated.

IS THE WORD "THE WORD?"

Other seminarians and pastors began to decide whether to accept the whole Word as inspired by God or whether the Word can be interpreted through their own "brilliant" minds.

Paul had no such illusion. "All Scripture is God-breathed and is useful for teaching, rebuking, correcting and training in righteousness, so that the man of God may be thoroughly equipped for every good work," he wrote to Timothy (2 Tim. 3:16–17).

Peter even classified Paul's writings as "Scripture" in his second letter. "His [Paul's] letters contain some things that are hard to understand, which ignorant and unstable people distort, as they do the *other Scriptures*, to their own destruction" (2 Pet. 3:16, my emphasis).

If Jesus has been raised from the dead, we can be assured that He is able to keep for us those portions of Scripture that are trustworthy and able to lead us into His will. I choose to accept the whole Word as the "Word."

NO FIRE AND BRIMSTONE?

This casual acceptance of the Bible that allows us to re-interpret Scripture continues to move into our own era.

"Is there a hell?"

"No! The Lord is too merciful to send anyone to a place of eternal fire! This passage is not meant to be taken literally."

But what does Jesus say?

"Then he will say to those on his left, 'Depart from me, you who are cursed, into the eternal fire prepared for the devil and his angels'.... then they will go away to eternal punishment" (Matt. 25:41, 46).

"If your hand causes you to sin, cut if off. It is better for you to enter life maimed than with two hands to go into hell, where the fire never goes out... if your eye causes you to sin, pluck it out. It is better for you to enter the kingdom of God with one eye than to have two eyes and be thrown into hell, where 'their worm does not die and the fire is not quenched'" (Mark 9:43, 47).

Pretty convincing evidence for a literal hell, wouldn't you say? If Jesus chooses to fulfill His words figuratively rather than literally, I will rejoice, but His words are obviously intended to keep us from the worst place we can imagine, a place described as fire, hell, eternal punishment, outer darkness, where "the worms that eat them do not die and the fire is not quenched" (Mark 9:48).

I choose not to ignore the warnings.

QUENCH THE SPIRIT?

Actively debated in some Christian circles is the work of the Holy Spirit. Are spiritual gifts still valid for today? Does God still do the same kind of miracles that are recorded in Scripture? Does the Holy Spirit speak to us? What about people who claim to have seen angels or who have had visions or dreams that are interpreted as coming from God. A prominent teacher in the United States recently published a book in which he claimed that most if not all of today's Holy Spirit claims are not a work of God, but a deception. Perhaps this man has experienced the excesses that may come from those who claim to be walking in the Spirit, but whose lives are devoid of the Spirit's fruit, but we must never allow others to shape our relationship to Jesus and His Spirit.

My Bible still teaches me that it is the "mind controlled by the Spirit" (Rom. 8:6) that brings life and peace, that "if anyone does not have the Spirit of Christ, he does not belong to Christ" (v.9), and that only through the Spirit of God dwelling in me will I be able to "put to death the misdeeds of the body" (v. 13).

I am also clearly instructed to "eagerly desire spiritual gifts, especially the gift of prophecy" (1 Cor. 14:1), to "live by the Spirit," to "keep in step with the Spirit" in order to produce "the fruit of the Spirit" (Gal. 5:16, 25 and 22), just as I am further counseled not to "grieve the Holy Spirit of God" (Eph. 4:30) nor to "put out the Spirit's fire" (1 Thess. 5:19).

Rather than using my energy to criticize those who are pressing in to experience more of God's Spirit, and pointing to excesses that may not be 100 percent pure Spirit, I'd rather use my energy desiring to be "filled with the Spirit" (Eph. 5:18), to be one who asks, knowing that I have a Father in heaven who will "give the Holy Spirit to those who ask him" (Luke 11:13), so that I am so filled with the Spirit that "rivers of living water will flow from within [me]" (John 7:38).

HOLY UNIONS?

Many church leaders in our generation have decided that sexual love between two men or two women can be holy and that such committed relationships and unions should be celebrated and blessed in our churches. They contend that such couples should receive the same privileges of marriage that one man-one woman couples have received since the Creation, and that these men or women can be equally ordained in church leadership roles in our churches and seminaries.

According to a report in the August 21, 2009, *Star Tribune*, the largest Lutheran church body in the United States, The Evangelical Lutheran Church of America approved the ordination of non-celibate gays to become ordained ministers. The vote passed by a vote of 559 to 451.[9]

On May 8, 2010, The General Assembly of The Presbyterian Church USA, the largest U.S. Presbyterian body, voted similarly by a margin of 372 to 323. The measure required ratification by a majority vote among the 173 Presbyteries before taking effect, an action that transpired on May 10, 2011.[10]

In an article entitled "Episcopal Church Approves Same-Sex Marriage, 'Transgender' Clergy," dated July 11, 2012, the Episcopal Church, in a 111–41 vote by their House of Bishops had passed a similar ordinance. The House of Deputies gave their approval by 78 percent of their voting lay members and 76 percent of their clergy.[11]

The very influential and effective World Vision organization issued a statement in March 2014, that they would employ "married" men or "married" women in their workforce. The outcry was so significant among their supporters that they reversed their decision within forty-eight hours, but the fact that their board had made the decision in the first place still shows a lack of biblical knowledge and application.

My Bible says, "Do not have sexual relationships with a man as one does with a woman; that is detestable" (Lev. 18:22; see also 20:13—some translations call this an "abomination.")

You say, "But that's from the Old Testament!"

True, but Paul told the Romans, at a time when sexual deviation was rampant in Roman society, "God gave them over in the sinful desires of their hearts to sexual impurity for the degrading of their bodies with one another….God gave them over to shameful lusts. Even their women exchanged natural relations for unnatural ones. In the same way the men also abandoned natural relations with women and were inflamed with lust for one another. Men committed indecent acts with other men, and received in themselves the due penalty for their perversion" (Rom. 1:21, 24, 26–27).

But what if the same-sex attraction is so strong that it cannot be overcome? What then?

Paul spoke to that as well. In writing to the Corinthians, he said, "Do not be deceived: Neither the sexually immoral nor idolaters nor adulterers *nor male prostitutes nor homosexual offenders* nor thieves nor the greedy nor drunkards nor slanderers nor swindlers will inherit the kingdom of God. And *that is what some of you were. But you were washed, you were sanctified, you were justified in the name of the Lord Jesus Christ and by the Spirit of our God"* (1 Cor. 6:9–11, emphasis mine).

Perversion or blessing? Which do we choose? The Word of God or the word of man?

But what about those who did not choose their orientation and who, even from earliest childhood, have had sexual attractions for the same sex? We love them unconditionally. The biblical commandment never gives permission to hate people. But we also challenge these to choose a lifestyle of obedience to God's way, just as we challenge each other to overcome desires and temptations that are not in accord with the will of God, and to be reshaped into His image.

> Which do we choose? The Word of God or the word of man?

KILL THE CHILD?

Much of today's church culture accepts the practice of killing children inside their mothers' wombs. If a woman becomes pregnant, whether married or unmarried, and she has no desire to have a child, or the pregnancy comes at an inconvenient time, kill the child! Or go to a legal professional whose business is killing children in their mothers' wombs.

You may object that this is not yet a "child" at all, rather a "fetus."

But my Book calls life in a mother's womb, a "child"—a "baby."

"Rebekah became pregnant. The *babies* jostled each other within her" (Gen. 25:22).

"When Elizabeth heard Mary's greeting, the *baby* leaped in her womb" (Luke 1:41). "As soon as the sound of your greeting reached my ears, the *baby* in *my womb* leaped for joy" (v. 44).

Baby or fetus? Let God decide!

If this seems like strong even unkind language, remember that Jesus came to redeem all of us from sin. Many who have intentionally had children destroyed inside the womb have repented and live gloriously free lives in Jesus, even rejoicing for the time when they will see that unborn child again in the arms of Jesus.

REJECT THE JEWS?

Millions in the Church tell me that God is finished with Israel and that the blessings intended for Israel and the Jewish people have now been relegated to the church. Present-day Israel has nothing to do with prophecy—pure happenstance. If Jewish people are to come to Jesus, they should leave their Jewishness, become Christians, and join our churches.

I have in my file a letter from a pastor who believes that the modern State of Israel has nothing to do with prophecy. "I received...your impressive literature...and your firm conviction that the modern State of Israel is a fulfillment of prophecy. The Christian church today is awash in this type of teaching, and you will rarely meet someone as old-fashioned as I who believes it to be false teaching and a corruption of Scripture."

Unfortunately, my friend's opinion is not all that rare. Much of the Church today does not consider today's Israel a fulfillment of prophecy.

But my Bible specifically states that a time would come when the Jewish people would return not only from the east—that would have been from Babylon—but also from the south, west and north. At no other time in history has this happened. The modern State of Israel is a reuniting of Abraham, Isaac, and Israel's descendants from over one hundred nations from the four corners of the earth.

Isaiah prophesied, "I will bring your children from the east and gather you from the west. I will say to the north, 'Give them up!' and to the south, 'Do not hold them back.' Bring my sons from afar and my daughters from the ends of the earth" (43:5–6).

The West—from European nations, the Americas, and as far away as Australia and New Zealand.

The South—Ethiopia and other African nations, with many thousands, particularly in Ethiopia in refugee camps awaiting their time of return.

The North—Russia from the far north refused for decades to allow their Jewish people to return, but that all changed in the late 20th century when over one million Russian Jews came out of exile back to their ancient home, so that the Russian language has become a major second language of Israel.

Today's Israel clearly fulfills these ancient prophecies.

"(God) remembers his covenant forever, the word he commanded for a thousand generations," David sang, "the covenant he made with Abraham, the oath he swore to Isaac. He confirmed it to Jacob as a decree, to Israel as an everlasting covenant, 'To you I will give the land of Canaan as the portion you will inherit" (1 Chron. 16:15–18).

"His covenant!" "A thousand generations!" That's a long time—at least forty thousand years.

"Did God reject his people?" Paul much later inquires. "By no means!... Did they stumble so as to fall beyond recovery? Not at all! Rather, because of their transgression, salvation has come to the Gentiles to make Israel envious. But if their transgression means riches for the world, and their loss means riches for the Gentiles, how much greater riches will their fullness bring!…If their rejection is the reconciliation of the world, what will their acceptance be but life from the dead?" (Rom. 11:1, 11–12, 15).

Greater riches when Israel comes into her fullness! Their acceptance brings life from the dead? That's what the Book says!

Yes, deception is happening. "Even the elect..." if that were possible. "From your own number!"

A time for vigilance! In the Word! On our knees! A time to "watch out for those who cause divisions and put obstacles in your way that are contrary to the teaching you have learned. Keep away from them. For such people are not serving our Lord Christ, but their own appetites. By smooth talk and flattery they deceive the minds of naïve people" (Rom. 16:17–18). A time to repent of our own sinful actions and allow the Holy Spirit to use even our ungodly past as a testimony to His goodness and a challenge to others to embrace forgiveness and walk forward in great joy.

Deception is here and deception is coming, but this is not a time for fear! "The one who is in you is greater!" (1 John 4:4). His Spirit is within!

Righteousness is maturing! Everything is working for our good!
Those are His promises!

NOTES

1. "The Christianity of Hitler revealed in his speeches and proclamations," compiled by Jim Walker, Originated: 27 Feb. 1997, Additions: 03 Jun. 2006.
2. Eric Metaxas, *Bonhoeffer: Pastor, Martyr, Prophet, Spy* (Nashville, TN: Thomas Nelson, 2010), pp. 171, 174.
3. This is the summation of Luther's 1543 published work, *On the Jews and Their Lies*, included in a 1993 *Christianity Today* article by Dr. Eric W. Gritsch entitled, "Was Luther Anti-Semitic?" Dr. Gritsch was the Maryland Synod Professor of Church History at Lutheran Theological Seminary in Gettysburg, Pennsylvania, and the director of the Institute for Luther Studies.
4. From Timothy J. Keller's Foreword in Eric Metaxas's *Bonhoeffer*, p. 155.
5. Metaxas, *Seven Men* (Nashville, TN: Nelson Publishing, 2013), p. 102. This is the way Eric Metaxas describes Bonhoeffer's influence in Hitler's Germany.
6. Ibid., pp. 103–104.
7. Richard Wurmbrand, *Tortured for Christ* (Bartlesville, OK: Living Sacrifice Book Company. First published by The Voice of the Martyrs, formerly called Christian Mission to the Communist World, Inc., 1967), p. 15.
8. Ibid., pp. 15–16.
9. http://www.startribune.com/lifestyle/faith.
10. http://www.christianpost.com/article/20100709/pcusa-assembly-oks-removing-gay-ordination-ban/index.html
11. This statement is quoted in the article by Dave Bohon in the online New American, although there were multiple news agencies that gave the same report.

CHAPTER 8

WELCOME THE KING!

Look, he is coming with the clouds.
~Revelation 1:7

I just made a trip to the airport, not to depart on some international flight, as I often do, but because some friends of mine were arriving and I wanted to welcome them to our city. "Should we get a taxi when we arrive?" they had suggested...but that would have been inconceivable. They were our honored guests! We left our home in order to meet them and welcome them.

The apostle John describes the scene surrounding Lazarus's death. When Lazarus became ill, the sisters sent word to Jesus, knowing that He could heal their brother (see John 11:21, 32). Jesus intentionally delayed his return to Bethany because He anticipated the glory that would come to God through Lazarus's resurrection (see v. 4).

Four days later, Martha learned that Jesus was outside the city. She left her home, later joined by Mary, to greet Him and bring Him back with them. Why? Why not wait until Jesus arrived at their home? Unthinkable! They rushed out to meet Jesus because He was their beloved friend, the One who could help them, and they couldn't wait to see Him!

When Paul was taken prisoner by the Romans and was being brought to Rome for trial, Luke was a part of the group accompanying Paul. He records the reception they were given outside the city: "The brothers there had heard that we were coming, and they traveled as far as the Forum of Appius and the Three Taverns to meet us" (Acts 28:15).

Traveled as far as the Forum of Appius and the Three Taverns? Obviously quite a distance! Why? Why not wait in Rome for Paul to arrive? They would then have plenty of time to visit with him. Not a chance! Paul was a highly respected leader, and the brothers wanted to give him a proper reception, even though he was being escorted by armed Roman guards.

Why do today's politicians make such a production of receiving heads of state, often including an extensive motorcade to the airport? Why not rather remain in their residences and await the arrival of their honored guests? Unacceptable! Such a breach of etiquette could begin a major world conflict.

Jesus told the story of ten virgins. "At that time," he said, "the kingdom of heaven will be like ten virgins who took their lamps and went out to meet the bridegroom" (Matt. 25:1).

They did not wait for Him (the Bridegroom/Jesus) to come to them. They went out to meet Him!

WELCOMING PARTY?

It is important that we remember this protocol as we read about Jesus' return to earth and believers going up to meet Him in the sky.

"The Lord himself will come down from heaven (1 Thess. 4:16). "God will bring with Jesus those who have fallen asleep in him" (v. 14). "We who are still alive…will certainly not precede those who have fallen asleep" (v. 15). "We will be caught up with them in the clouds" (v. 17).

Jesus is on His way back when the saints from ages past and those still alive at His coming will rise to meet him.

Are we to assume that Jesus pauses in mid-air, gathers the saints together, only to do a round trip back to heaven with those who have joined Him? Not likely. Is it not rather that we are meeting Him in order to bring Him back to reign upon earth for an unprecedented thousand-year time of peace, as both Zechariah (14:3–9) and John (Rev. 20:1–6) predict?

According to Paul, believers who die are immediately with the Lord, and will accompany Him when He returns (see Phil. 1:23 and 1 Thess. 4:14). The writer of Ecclesiastes tells us that the body, made of dust, "returns to the ground it came from, and the spirit returns to God who gave it" (12:7). Paul explains that the saints still living will not "sleep, but...will all be changed – in a flash, in the twinkling of an eye, at the last trumpet...the dead will be raised imperishable, and we will be changed" (1 Cor. 15:51–52).

Could it be that the much-anticipated "rapture" of the church is simply proper protocol—a welcoming party for the King? Is it possible that we are with Him in the air only as a welcoming committee for His return?

Is this not like my trip to the airport, like Mary and Martha's leaving their home to meet Jesus, the brothers in Rome traveling a great distance to greet Paul, or the bridesmaids going to meet the groom? Will it not be our great joy to rise to meet our Honored Guest—who is no guest at all, but is Earth's Returning Ruler? We will hear the trumpet, we will respond to the call of the archangel, we will leave homes and graves, receive our resurrection bodies, and ascend to welcome the King.

RESURRECTION BODIES

All of this will remain somewhat a mystery until the full revelation comes. But one thing seems clear. We—both those from past generations who have risen from the dead, as well as those of us who are still alive at His coming—will receive new bodies.

> Could it be that the much-anticipated "rapture" of the church is simply proper protocol—a welcoming party for the King?

What about this resurrection body? What relationship does the new body have with the one we've used so long on earth? Will we recognize each other? What kind of body will the new one be?

Paul was appreciative of this kind of curiosity. In writing to the believers in Corinth, he posed the same kinds of questions we are asking: "How are the dead raised? With what kind of body will they come?" (1 Cor. 15:35).

Then Paul began to offer this explanation: "What you sow does not come to life unless it dies. When you sow, you do not plant the body that will be, but just a seed....God gives it a body as he has determined.... So will it be with the resurrection of the dead. The body that is sown is perishable, it is raised imperishable...it is sown in weakness, it is raised in power; it is sown a natural body, it is raised a spiritual body....The first man was of the dust of the earth, the second man from heaven...just as we have borne the likeness of the earthly man, so shall we bear the likeness of the man from heaven" (vv. 37–38, 42–44, 47–49).

I have a package of carnation seeds in one of my desk drawers. I keep it there to take to burials. Using Paul's analogy, I like to compare the disintegrating seed (our dead and decaying body) to the beauty and fragrance of the flower when it blooms (the body that will be raised incorruptible). I want people to understand Paul's comparison of the seed to what the seed produces.

No hostess ever decorated her table with a bowl of carnation seeds. But let those seeds die, and the blossoms that result will be used to adorn the world's most festive dinner tables!

That's Paul's description of the resurrection body. Somehow the resurrection body that will be raised up from our earthly body is as different as the carnation seed and the flower. And yet, that resurrection body is connected to the body that turned to dust so that we will be recognizable.

How do I know that? We have heaven's own exhibition of what a resurrection body will look like.

HEAVEN'S EXHIBIT "A"

We need only to consider Jesus, His death and resurrection. Three days after His death, His body was missing from the tomb, so Jesus' resurrection body is, in some way, connected to the one He had used while on the earth. And yet, this new body was different. In some cases, even His closest friends did not immediately recognize him.

That happened on Resurrection morning when He began a conversation with Mary Magdalene. "She turned around and saw Jesus standing there, but she did not realize that it was Jesus" (John 20:14)—not until He called her name.

Later that day, the same thing happened to Cleopas and his friend as they were walking on the road to Emmaus. While discussing the events of the recent Crucifixion and their dashed hope that Jesus was the Messiah, they looked up to see Him, but He "appeared in a different form"

(Mark 16:12). The three of them walked for some distance together, their conversation centering around the events of the past days, before they realized to whom they were speaking.

Jesus quoted passages from Moses and the prophets, explaining "to them what was said in all the Scriptures concerning himself" (Luke 24:27). Not until He went into the house with them, "took bread, gave thanks, broke it and began to give it to them" (v. 30) were their eyes suddenly opened so that they recognized Him. But just as suddenly, "he disappeared from their sight" (v. 31).

Cleopas and his friend quickly made their way back to Jerusalem to tell the rest of the disciples what had happened. "While they were still talking about this, Jesus himself stood among them and said to them, 'Peace be with you'" (v. 36).

This so frightened the disciples that they thought they were seeing a ghost (see v. 37)! And even though Jesus showed them the scars in His hands and feet, they were still not convinced that this was a real live Person in front of them. Not until He asked for something to eat, they gave Him a piece of broiled fish, and "he took it and ate it in their presence" (vv. 42–43), were they sure this was really Jesus in a resurrected body who stood before them.

Jesus' appearance in a room where "the doors (were) locked for fear" (John 20:19) seems to have been repeated several times. Over the next forty days, He appeared and disappeared at will, sometimes to only one or two people. On another occasion, He revealed Himself to His disciples on the shore of the Galilee while they were fishing (see John 21). And at least once, He showed up before a crowd of as many as five hundred (see 1 Cor. 15:6).

During these appearances, He continually "spoke about the kingdom of God" (Acts 1:3). He told the disciples to stay in Jerusalem until Holy Spirit power came upon them. They would then begin a proclamation that would ultimately reach to the ends of the earth (v. 8).

And then one day, Jesus went out to the Mount of Olives "in the vicinity of Bethany" where "he lifted up his hands and blessed them," and "while he was blessing them, he left them and was taken up into heaven" (Luke 24:50–51).

As the disciples gazed with yearning toward the sky, two angels standing nearby reassured them that He would return to earth "in the same way you have seen him go" (Acts 1:11) – a return that is yet to happen.

So, what will we be able to do in our resurrection bodies? We can walk, talk, and eat just as we can in our present bodies. We can appear and disappear through closed and locked doors. (I wonder if we will be able to travel at the speed of thought!) We can appear in different forms. We may still carry some of the scars from our old body, but I would assume that Jesus' scars served only to glorify the Father and to prove to His friends that He was indeed the same Jesus who had been beaten, crucified, and buried. (I rather suspect that our resurrection bodies may not be scarred in any way. But if they are, those scars will also glorify the Lord.)

Our resurrection bodies will be gloriously beautiful. Don't forget Paul's description: "Sown in dishonor...raised in power...sown perishable...raised imperishable...sown in weakness... raised in power... sown a natural body...raised a spiritual body!"

And don't ever forget the difference between the carnation seed and the flower!

KING OF THE UNIVERSE

"The LORD will be king over the whole earth. On that day there will be one LORD, and his name the only name," Zechariah predicted so many centuries ago (14:9). "The LORD my God will come, and all the holy ones with him" (v. 5). "The Lord Jesus (will be) revealed from heaven...with his powerful angels," Paul echoed a few decades after Jesus' ascension (2 Thess. 1:7).

> Saints and angels— all a part of the King's entourage!

Saints and angels—all a part of the King's entourage! Those who have died and those who are still alive! "According to the Lord's own word... we who are still alive, who are left till the coming of the Lord, will certainly not precede those who have fallen asleep," Paul assured the Thessalonians (4:15). At the same time, heaven bursts open with, "Hallelujah! Salvation and glory and power belong to our God...For our Lord God Almighty reigns. Let us rejoice and be glad and give him glory! For the wedding of the Lamb has come, and his bride has made herself ready" (Rev. 19:1, 6–7). And all the inhabitants of the earth?

Still reeling from the earthquake on the Mount of Olives, they will be watching as the Eastern Gate of the Old City of Jerusalem splits the Muslim cemetery just outside that gate wide open. This gate, the Beautiful Gate (see Acts 3:2), is the one through which Jesus and His friends so frequently walked on their way to the Mount of Olives and to the home of their friends Mary, Martha, and Lazarus in Bethany.

THE EASTERN GATE WILL OPEN

Centuries before Jesus arrived the first time, Ezekiel prophesied about that Eastern gate: "The gate...the one facing east...was shut. The LORD said to me, 'This gate is to remain shut. It must not be opened; no one may enter through it. It is to remain shut because the LORD, the God of Israel, has entered through it. The prince himself is the only one who may sit inside the gateway to eat in the presence of the LORD. He is to enter by way of the portico of the gateway and go out the same way'" (44:1–3).

Interesting! Why is this Eastern Gate the only gate of the Old City that has been closed for centuries? The man who ordered it closed was fulfilling the very prophecy he was trying to prevent. In the year 1517, when Suleiman the Magnificent conquered Jerusalem, he rebuilt the city walls, but ordered the Eastern Gate sealed. Why? The story goes that he had heard of Ezekiel's prophecy and conferred with some of the rabbis about their belief in the coming Messiah. When he heard that the Messiah was to enter through the Eastern Gate, he ordered the gate closed, even putting a Muslim cemetery in front of the Gate, knowing that no Jewish Messiah would defile Himself by walking through a Muslim cemetery.

THE DEAD SEA WILL THRIVE

Another amazing geographical event happens on the Day when Jesus returns. Both Zechariah and Ezekiel speak of living water that begins to flow from Jerusalem, "out from under the threshold of the temple toward the east" (Ezek. 47:1)...half to the eastern sea and half to the western sea" (Zech.14:8). "The water was coming down from under the south side of the temple, south of the altar" (Ezek. 47:2), and finally emptying into the

Dead Sea (see v. 8).

This living water that begins with a trickle from under the Temple—then ankle deep, knee deep, waist deep, and finally "deep enough to swim in – a river that no one could cross" (v. 5)—makes everything fresh. The salt water of the Dead Sea becomes fresh. Fruit trees line the banks on both sides of what has now become a river. "Their leaves will not wither, nor will their fruit fall. Every month they will bear, because the water from the sanctuary flows to them. Their fruit will serve for food and their leaves for healing" (v. 12).

PEACE WILL PREVAIL

Ezekiel's prophecy seems to have a double fulfillment. The first, when Jesus returns to reign over a world of peace for a thousand years (see Rev. 20:1–7), a time when people live long lives, but death has not yet been defeated (see Isa. 65:20). The second, the final destiny of redeemed mankind, when we enter into eternity future, and the saved of Adam's children again have access to the "Tree of Life" and live forever (see Gen. 34:3, and Rev. 22:1–5).

Both Micah and Isaiah foresee a time of world peace when swords will be beaten into plowshares, and spears into pruning hooks, since "nation will not take up sword against nation, nor will they train for war anymore" (Isa. 2:4; Micah 4:3). "Every man will sit under his own vine and under his own fig tree, and no one will make them afraid" (Mic. 4:4).

The world peace of which the prophets speak affects not only men and nations and swords and pruning hooks—not only a time when men sit under their own fig trees and enjoy sweet fellowship with God and with each other—but even the animal kingdom is affected by the King's return. Adam's generations, sons and daughters of the one who gave all the animals their names in the first place (see Gen. 2:19), are restored to fellowship with the animals, and the animals with each other—the wild and the tame living together in peace.

"The wolf will live with the lamb, the leopard will lie down with the goat, the calf and the lion and the yearling together; and a little child will lead them. The cow will feed with the bear, their young will lie down together, and the lion will eat straw like the ox. The infant will play near the hole of the cobra, and the young child put his hand into the viper's nest. They will neither harm nor destroy on all my holy mountain, for the earth will be full of the knowledge of the LORD as the waters cover the sea" (Isa. 11:6–9).

I don't know about you, but I look forward to that day. I've stroked and brushed a horse's mane and ridden bareback across open fields, but lions? I keep telling all the children that I'll jump on a lion's back, they on the backs of tigers, and we'll challenge each other to a race!

I assume also that we will be energetic until we are, let's say, six or seven hundred years old. Isaiah says, "As the days of a tree, so will be the days of my people" (65:22). It seems to me that we are restored to the pre-Flood days when centenarians are considered young. "He who dies at a hundred will be considered accursed" (v. 20).

This will be a remarkable time. The devil himself has been "seized," "bound," thrown "into the Abyss…(where he is) locked and sealed" for a thousand years (Rev. 20:1–3). All the nations will soon learn that, in order to thrive, and especially if they want to continue to have rainfall, they will need to send representatives to the Feast of Tabernacles in Jerusalem annually "to worship the King who is the LORD Almighty" (Zech. 14:16).

Do you begin to understand why Paul, contemplating the future when Jesus would return, told the Thessalonians, "Encourage each other with these words" (1 Thess. 4:18)?

This is also the reason I can keep believing and encouraging others to believe that, regardless of how difficult the times may become, there is victory ahead! The King is coming, and He works everything for our good!

RECEIVE YOUR INHERITANCE!

*Inherit the kingdom prepared for you from
the foundation of the world.*
~Matthew 25:34

I smile every time I think about the future millennial kingdom and eternity future. We need to pay more attention to the closing chapters of John's Revelation and parallel Scriptures that speak of those times to come. The biblical description of our future is far more than harps and clouds!

I'm convinced that, in our desire to close off ungodly imaginations of lust, pride, or greed, we have shut down Godly imaginations. Yes, "God saw that the wickedness of man was great…and that every imagination of the thoughts of his heart was only evil continually" (Gen. 6:5 KJV). Yes, because of man's evil propensity for being "vain in their imaginations" (Rom. 1:21), God gave them over to their own ungodliness. Yes, we are encouraged to "cast[ing] down imaginations, and every high thing that exalteth itself against the knowledge of God" (2 Cor 10:5 KJV).

On the other hand, Jesus continually evoked imagination through the parables He taught, in His descriptions of the "Son of Man coming on the clouds of the sky, with power and great glory" (Matt. 24:30), and through many other vivid depictions of the Father's relationship with us.

Paul specifically encouraged Godly imagination when writing to the Ephesians. After pouring out a prayer for power in the Holy Spirit, for supernatural love to be grasped, then challenging us to come into the fullness of Jesus' nature, he ends with this outburst of praise: "To him who is able to do immeasurably more than all we ask or *imagine*, according to his power that is at work within us, to him be glory!" (3:20, emphasis mine).

More than we can *imagine!*

The most effective way to rid ourselves of ungodly imaginations is to fill our minds with Godly imaginations. Darkness is not expelled by concentrating on the darkness, but by bringing light into the equation.

Reclaim your Godly imagination!

GODLY IMAGINATION

Imagine a perfect, all-wise king ruling a world at peace. Imagine that the King is Jesus who sits enthroned in Jerusalem, the center of world government, with heads of states and leaders from every nation coming to Jerusalem to honor Him. "A king will reign in righteousness and rulers will rule with justice," Isaiah foresaw (32:1). "Kings...of distant shores will bring tribute to [the King]...and present him gifts. All kings will bow down to him and all nations will serve him" (Ps. 72:10–11).

> Darkness is not expelled by concentrating on the darkness, but by bringing light into the equation.

There will be no longer a need for United Nations meetings, where men and women sit around tables conjuring up peace plans. No more evil dictators. Not even elected officials who, with all good intentions, seem never able to bring about those hoped-for changes. At the head of our government will be a Perfect King with perfect laws interpreted by a Supreme Court of judges who were Jesus' closest friends on the earlier visit (see Matt. 19:28).

Imagine Jerusalem as the headquarters of this unusual government, the Temple of God situated at its highest elevation, and Jerusalem itself as "chief among the mountains...raised above the hills...all nations" streaming to it (Isa. 2:2)—people all over the world encouraging each other to make that trip to Jerusalem. "Come, let us go up to the mountain of the LORD...He will teach us his ways, so that we may walk in his paths" (v. 3). "Let us go at once to entreat the LORD...I myself am going" (Zech. 8:21).

"This is the place of my throne and the place for the soles of my feet," God told Ezekiel in speaking of the future temple. "This is where I will live among the Israelites forever" (Ezek. 43:7).

Imagine those "who are still alive, who are left till the coming of the Lord" (1 Thess. 4:15), along with the "dead in Christ [who will] rise, (v. 16), being "caught up together [with Jesus] in the air" (v. 17) occupying the same time and space at the time when Jesus returns to become "King over the whole earth" (Zech. 14:9).

Imagine that those who have survived the upheaval that accompanied His return (see Zech. 14:1–8) being restored to long lives as in the days of Noah, when "never again will there be... an infant who lives but a few days, or an old man who does not live out his years; he who fails to reach a hundred will be considered accursed... as the days of a tree so will be the days of my people" (Isa. 65:20–22).

THE JEWISH PEOPLE SOUGHT AFTER!

Imagine Jewish people becoming the most sought-after people group on earth, constantly expressing their allegiance to Yeshua, to Jesus, the returned King whom they now recognize as the Son of David, Son of God, "Mighty God, Everlasting Father, Prince of Peace" (Isa. 9:6). Jewish people will become the most popular people on the planet: "Ten men from all languages and nations will take firm hold of one Jew by the hem of his robe and say, 'Let us go with you, because we have heard that God is with you'" (v. 23).

Imagine the synagogues of the world as centers of Jesus-worship!

Imagine a world where holiness is the norm! What the first Adam forfeited in the Garden, the "last Adam"..."the second man" restored (1 Cor. 15:45, 47).

Imagine a world with no oppression and no violence (see Ps. 72:13–14), where "the righteous will flourish; [and] prosperity will abound till the moon is no more" (v. 7).

Imagine a world of nations with no war machines and no armies (see. Isa. 2:4).

Recapture Godly imagination!

PRECURSOR OF THINGS TO COME?

The small town of Almalonga, Guatemala, experienced a foretaste of Jesus' millennial reign a few years ago when the town of 20,000 inhabitants went through a major transformation. For four hundred years, the town had been seen as a "pit of poverty," plagued with demon worship, alcoholism, and extreme drought. Four jails were in constant use to maintain some semblance of order.

But a few passionate followers of Jesus accepted the challenge to see the city transformed, moved there, and began to preach the gospel. Person after person responded, the demon powers were challenged and silenced, so that by the year 2000, over 95 percent of the population had turned their lives over to Jesus and the whole area was experiencing renewal. Within a very short time, underground springs opened up, and lush gardens were producing vegetables that became the focus of the Department of Agriculture and got the attention of believers from around the world. Huge carrots the size of forearms and cabbages of enormous proportions can be seen in a video entitled "Transformation I," produced by the Sentinel Group. Almalonga is now called the "Garden Spot of Guatemala."[1]

Recapture Godly imagination!

Imagine this kind of transformation in every city and every nation of the world! "Every tribe and language and people and nation" (Rev. 5:9) will be a part of the ultimate victory and will surround the Lord's throne, God assured John.

THE FINAL BATTLE

Only one hurdle stands between this last great era of world peace and eternity future when Adam's redeemed children are with the Lord forever. As the millennial reign comes to an end, Satan will be released from his thousand-year imprisonment, and, with all his pent-up fury, will engage the world in one last attempt to overthrow God's government and establish himself as the supreme world ruler. For whatever reasons, he is released "to deceive the nations in the four corners of the earth" (Rev. 20:8) once again. For those who have come to faith in Jesus during the thousand years, one last test of faith will come. Satan's forces go throughout the earth, ultimately surrounding "the camp of God's people, the city he loves" (v. 9) in one final demonic gasp. His attack is, thankfully, short-lived. "Fire came down from heaven and devoured them. And the devil...was thrown into the lake of burning sulfur...(to) be tormented day and night for ever and ever" (v. 10).

JUDGMENT OF BELIEVERS: "NOT GUILTY!"

With the demise of Satan, world attention turns to the judgment scene where all are judged "according to what they had done as recorded in the books" (Rev. 20:12). Believers can stand confidently before the Judge, not because of their own righteous deeds, but because they have accepted Him whose righteousness has been imparted to them on the basis of faith (see Rom. 3:20–21), and because our adversary has been vanquished and our Advocate is not only our Defender, but has taken the punishment that should have been given to us. Ours is not a judgment of condemnation, but a judgment of assignment for the coming eternal kingdom.

In one of Jesus' kingdom parables, the returning king gave one servant "charge of ten cities" while another was given "charge of five cities" (Luke 19:17–19)—same eternal blessing, different assignments.

For those who have refused salvation, whose "name was not found written in the book of life," John sees a horrifying end. "If anyone's name was not found written in the book of life, he was thrown into the lake of fire" (Rev. 20:15), a place never intended for Adam's children, yet the destiny of those who have refused salvation (see John 3:17, 36). In another of Jesus' stories, the King condemns the disobedient to the "eternal fire prepared [not for mankind, but] for the devil and his angels" (Matt. 25:41).

ETERNITY FUTURE

Following the judgment scene, the ultimate intention for man at the Creation will finally be reached—God and man living together, face to face, in total unity for all eternity in "a new heaven and a new earth"

(Rev. 21:1). This is not a make-believe earth and heaven, but an earth that is reunited with heaven as in the Garden at the beginning. This new earth still has cities and nations with kings. We serve and we reign with the Lord on this new and perfect earth forever and ever.

God tells us very little about eternity future, but seems to encourage us with wild imagination. In the closing visions of John's Revelation, he sees the new Jerusalem, the place Jesus had promised to prepare (see John 14:1), "coming down out of heaven from God" (21:2). A loud voice from the throne was heard: "Now the dwelling of God is with men, and he will live with them....God himself will be with them and be their God. He will wipe away every tear from their eyes. There will be no more death or mourning or crying or pain, for the old order of things has passed away" (vv. 3–4).

This is good! Imagine a place with no death, no grief, no pain. No longer do we simply live long lives as in the pre-Flood era and in the millennium, but we live forever in a place of perfection.

The new Jerusalem is no small, ordinary city. It is 1400 miles (2200 kilometers), "in length and as wide and high as it is long" (v. 16). By today's measurements, the city itself would cover all the land originally given to Abraham for his descendants (see Gen. 15:18–21), but the city is also as high as it is long and wide—almost 300 times as high as our planes fly through the skies! Why such a height unless there is some use for it? Are we able to ascend into the heavens as well as walk with both feet on the earth? We can only imagine. We do know that the city shines "with the glory of God and its brilliance...like that of a very precious jewel" (Rev. 21:11).

The new Jerusalem is well connected to its past. The names of Israel's twelve tribes are inscribed on its twelve gates (v. 12), with the names of the "twelve apostles of the Lamb" engraved on foundation stones of finest gems (see vv. 19–20). Each of the gates of the city is fashioned from a "single pearl...the street of the city...of pure gold" (v. 21).

"Nothing impure will ever enter" into the city or its nations, "nor will anyone who does what is shameful or deceitful" (v. 27). God Himself and the Lamb provide both Temple and light (see vv. 22–23).

"The river of the water of life, as clear as crystal," (22:1) flows from the throne down the middle of the great street of the city. On each side of the river is the "tree of life, bearing twelve crops of fruit, yielding its fruit every month. And the leaves of the tree are for the healing of the nations" (v. 2). We've seen this river before! And we've seen this Tree of Life!

The tree from which Adam and Eve were not allowed to eat has been restored to Adam's children. God's mercy did not allow Adam and Eve, in their fallen state, to "reach out (their hands) and take...from the tree of life and eat, and live forever" (Gen. 3:22). Not even during the millennium was mankind afforded this opportunity. Those trees along the river flowing from underneath the Temple were similar to these, but this time, those who eat will live forever.

In the last recorded Scripture from Jesus' own mouth, He says, "Blessed are those who wash their robes, that they may have the right to the tree of life and may go through the gates into the city" (Rev. 22:14).

God's "servants will serve him," John tells us, and "they will reign for ever and ever" (vv. 3–5).

How will we serve? Over what will we reign? Much of this is left to our imagination, but Paul assures us that our imagination is not big enough to embrace all that God has in mind for us. "Immeasurably more than all we ask or imagine" were his words to the Ephesians.

"Encourage each other with these words" (1 Thess. 4:18), Paul admonished when talking about our future, but how can we encourage each other if we never ponder what the future holds?

And never forget that though the process of entering into the millennial reign of peace and into the ultimate eternity of love, joy and peace may not always be easy, we are assured that He will continue to work all of it for the ultimate good of those who love Him and are His called ones.

Never forget!

NOTES

1. Jim Rutz, "City Transformation on a Scale not Seen Before," *World Net Daily*, June 21, 2005.

CHAPTER 10

READ THE BOOK!

The word of God is living and active.
~Hebrews 4:12

On Sunday, March 27, 1977, in the most deadly aviation disaster in history, two Boeing 747s collided on the Tenerife airport runway in the Canary Islands. The planes immediately burst into flames, killing all 248 on board the KLM flight 4805 that had originated in Amsterdam, and 335 of the 396 on board the Pan Am Flight 1736, out of Los Angeles.

One of the 61 survivors of the Pan Am flight was a man named Norman Williams, who, along with his fellow travelers, had embarked from L.A. on what was supposed to have been the vacation of a lifetime, a cruise that was to have begun on the Gran Canaria Island.

On the morning of the disaster, as Norman was about to leave for the airport, his prayer-warring mother began to weep, sensing that Norman could be in danger. She cautioned him to stand firmly on God's promises and protection.

All was well during the flight from Los Angeles to New York, where the Pan Am flight changed crews and picked up 14 additional passengers. The continuation of the journey to the Canary Islands was routine until they neared the islands. At 1:15 that afternoon, a terrorist bomb had exploded in the Gran Canaria International Airport terminal, causing all flights to be diverted to the nearby smaller Tenerife airport with only one runway. After almost four hours, the Gran Canaria airport reopened and the captain of the KLM flight, after what he thought was proper instruction from one of the two traffic controllers on duty, proceeded full throttle for takeoff, even though the Pan Am plane was still sitting at the other end of the runway. At 5:06 in the afternoon, the two jumbo jets collided. Flames immediately surrounded Norman Williams. At that exact moment, messages from Scripture began to fill Norman's mind:

"*I will never leave you nor forsake you.*"

"*Fear not!*"

"*I have summoned you by name and you are mine.*"

"*When you pass through the waters, I will be with you, and when you pass through the rivers, they will not sweep over you. When you walk through the fire, you will not be burned; the flames will not set you ablaze.*"

"I will not be burned!" Norman shouted. "The flames will not set me ablaze. I stand on the Word of God!" he continued. "I stand on the Word of God! I stand on the Word of God!"

At this point in some strange way—which Norman, to this day, cannot explain—he saw a hole in the ceiling of the cabin above him, was able to make his way to and through the hole, slide down the wing of the plane, and jump to safety.

He had read the Book!

Even though the bones in his left foot were shattered and he spent many days in recovery, neither he nor his clothes were burned. No other person in his area of the plane lived. Some of the bodies were charred beyond recognition.[1]

I met Norman when he accepted our invitation to bring his unusual testimony during a conference we sponsored in Nashville.

Why would words from the Bible be screaming in Norman's ears in his moment of danger? Because he had read the Book! Not just a casual read, but over a lifetime of devotion. These words had been his food.

Why did Jesus cry out from the cross, "My God, my God, why have you forsaken me?" Because the words from Psalm 22:1 were etched in his memory. Like a good Jewish boy, he had memorized much, or perhaps all of the Torah (the five books of Moses) and other Scriptures. Jesus, and in this case, Norman, was living the Book.

MEMORIZE THE WORD!

Years ago I downloaded Psalm 139 to my permanent memory file. I like to think of it that way instead of "memorizing Scripture." Memorizing is difficult; downloading may not be any easier, but it has a better ring to it. In fact, if I am not badly mistaken, it was on one of our Mt. Le Conte hikes when a young friend and I were walking the trail together, that he got the download. He wanted it (that's a first step). He was determined to get it (that's even better)!

So I would talk to the Lord out loud in the words of Psalm 139, and Michael would repeat after me:

"O Lord, you have searched me and you know me."
"O Lord, you have searched me and you know me."

"You know when I sit and when I rise."
"You know when I sit and when I rise."

"You perceive my thoughts from afar."
"You perceive my thoughts from afar."

"You discern my going out and my lying down;
  you are familiar with all my ways."

*"You discern my going out and my lying down;
  you are familiar with all my ways."*

"Search me, O God, and know my heart;…
  See if there is any offensive way in me,
  and lead me in the way everlasting."

*"Search me, O God, and know my heart;…
  See if there is any offensive way in me,
  and lead me in the way everlasting."*

Meditation and memorization are not quite the same, but they have the same outcome. Meditating is reflecting on something—a thought or an idea, some words or passages—thinking quietly, focusing on that one thing to the exclusion of everything else. Memorizing is thinking about certain words and phrases so long that they become a part of you. You learn them by heart! But you don't ever meditate on a psalm like this and stay the same.

I have had this 139th psalm living inside me for years, but one morning recently, I decided it was time to resurrect it. It had grown a bit rusty, so I went for a walk with it. Keeping carefully to the left side of the road to avoid the rush of early-morning traffic, I became lost in God. When I came to the phrase, "You have laid your hand upon me," it was as though I could feel His hand upon my head—anointing me, empowering me, encouraging me, directing me, assuring me. Tears began to stream from my eyes. All alone. In the traffic. On Graybar Lane near my house.

I began to wonder all over again why we believers do not spend more time meditating on God's Word, chewing on it, digesting it, absorbing it. I yearned for every person I know to have this life-altering experience. This is the way to overcome fear, anxiety, depression. His Word is true. His Word breathes life into us.

What was it the writer of Hebrews said? "The word of God is living and active. Sharper than any double-edged sword...it judges the thoughts and attitudes of the heart" (4:12).

And what did the psalmist say? "I have hidden your word in my heart that I might not sin against you" (119:11). Yes, that's it! His Word hidden, not on a bookshelf, nor even in my hands as I read it, but in my heart. Repeating His Word so much that it becomes a part of me. That's what "memorization" is—repeating a thing so many times that it is now locked inside you.

LIVE BY THE POWER OF THE WORD

Late in Paul's life, while imprisoned in Rome, he wrote a request to Timothy: "Do your best to come to me quickly," and "when you come, bring...my scrolls, especially the parchments" (2 Tim. 4:9, 13). Though death was near (see 4:8), and Paul had much of the Scripture inside him, he still needed the scrolls. He wanted more!

"The words I have spoken to you are spirit and they are life" Jesus told his disciples (John 6:63).

"Do not let this Word of Law depart from your mouth," God admonished Joshua as he was assuming the leadership of the nation of Israel (Josh. 1:8)

As we face the coming world upheavals, only those who read the Book and allow the words to permeate our hearts, absorbing them into our being, will be able to avoid deception. No amount of listening to our favorite preacher or television evangelist will assure that we are hearing truth. We need to read the Book for ourselves, then stand on its truth!

Our standing on the Word of God may not be as dramatic as that of Norman Williams, but it is essential that, as we approach the end of the age, we learn to depend upon the absolute validity of "the Book." Norman was spared from the destruction all around him because words from God were continually circulating inside of Him. You need that, too.

I challenge you to make His Word a part of your daily food. If you need a reading plan in which you never get behind, never get ahead, but assures you that, over time, you will read the Word through over and over again, then check the one I've used for years. You'll find it in Appendix D.

Yes, God works everything for good for those who love Him and are the called ones, but there are times when He cannot give us what He would like to give us because we have not prepared ourselves to receive.

Read the Book!

CHAPTER 11

PRAY THE WORD!

"When you pray..."
~Matthew 6:5

"You who remind the Lord, take no rest for yourselves; and give Him no rest until He establishes Jerusalem and makes her the praise of the earth" (Isa. 62:6–7 NASV).

Remind the Lord? Is He forgetful? Obviously not, but He wants us to take a stand on Scripture and not budge until the answer comes. James Goll suggests that the Lord is looking to us as His divine secretaries, to remind Him of His appointments, and of His promises.[1]

"No matter how many promises God has made, they are 'Yes' in Christ," Paul told the Corinthians. "And so through him the 'Amen' is spoken by us to the glory of God" (2 Cor. 1:20).

We speak the "Amen"! When we say, "Amen," we are actually saying, "Yes, Lord, I agree with that. It is established in Your Word. I believe it! I want that to be so in my life. So be it! Let it be done!"

There are promises God has given that do not come to fruition until we agree with those promises and, by faith, speak them into existence through our "Amen."

POSSIBILITY PRAYING

One verse changed my life several decades ago when I was crying out for greater victory and greater holiness. I was already keenly aware of my need for prayers of repentance. I had used those penitent prayers of David after Nathan confronted him about his sin with Bathsheba. I had etched those prayers onto my internal hard-drive and repeatedly sobbed them out before the Lord: "Against you, you only, have I sinned and done what is evil in your sight, so that you are proved right when you speak and justified when you judge....Cleanse me....Wash me....Create in me a pure heart!" (Ps. 51: 4, 7, 10). The prayers were cleansing, but I still had not gained the victory until the Lord showed me my destiny.

Because of childhood trauma (as so many of us have endured in one way or another), my mind was often involuntarily filled with mental debris. I was often tempted to give up hope of ever having a "pure heart" until I discovered a phrase out of Paul's letter to the Romans: "Those God foreknew he also predestined to be conformed to the likeness of his Son" (8:29).

I paused, stunned. Does this say what I think it says? God has a destiny for me (for us!)—we are "predestined to be conformed to the likeness of his Son?"

Is this possible? Predestined? My destiny is to be like Jesus?

Amen! I shouted in my loudest internal voice. *I, Don, am predestined to be like Jesus.*

My whole outlook on life changed in one Holy-Spirit-revelatory moment. I was suddenly on my way to becoming like Jesus. I had accepted God's promise. I had spoken the "Amen."

Within the following days, I found similar statements to confirm what I had come to believe.

"We, who with unveiled faces all reflect the Lord's glory, are being transformed into his likeness with ever-increasing glory, which comes from the Lord, who is the Spirit" (2 Cor. 3:18).

Amen!

We are "created to be like God in true righteousness and holiness" (Eph. 4:24).

Amen!

By participating with God, we become partakers "in the divine nature and escape the corruption in the world caused by evil desires" (2 Pet. 1:4).

Amen!

Soon after this discovery, in reading through John's first letter, I found another bit of truth that added weight to my journey: "If we confess our sins, he…will…purify us from all unrighteousness" (1 John 1:9).

This was good news since I had tried for years to be pure, to purify myself so that I could give God a pure self. It doesn't work that way. He is the one who purifies. My role is to receive His conviction, and confess.

What a deal! I thought. *Amen! Lord, You convict. I confess. You purify.*

From that day until this, I welcome the convicting voice of the Holy Spirit. One of His roles is "to convict the world of guilt" (John 16:8), Jesus told His friends. Over and over again I have experienced the victory that God gives when I obey, trusting His Word more than the way I feel.

IDENTIFICATIONAL REPENTANCE

In the waning years of the prophet Daniel's life, he had an experience that illustrates the way God desires us to relate to Scripture.

One day, while Daniel was reading from the Jeremiah scroll, his eyes landed on a prophecy whose time for fulfillment had come (just as we will do when we read His Word):

"When seventy years are completed for Babylon, I will come to you and fulfill my gracious promise to bring you back to this place" (29:10).

Seventy years, Daniel pondered. *It's been just about seventy years since King Nebuchadnezzar brought me to Babylon.*[2] *It is time for the captivity to end, time for us to return to Jerusalem!*

So what did Daniel do?

In his own way, he said, "Amen!"

He "turned to the Lord God and pleaded with him in prayer and petition, in fasting, and in sackcloth and ashes" (9:3).

He participated with God in the fulfillment of what God had spoken through one of His prophets. Daniel took upon himself, in what has come to be known as *identificational repentance and confession*, the sins of his people, and cried out to God: "We have sinned and done wrong. We have been wicked and have rebelled; we have turned away from your commands and laws. We have not listened to your servants the prophets, who spoke in your name to our kings, our princes and our fathers, and to all the people of the land" (vv. 5–6).

Though Daniel himself had done none of these things, he saw what God desired for his generation, spoke the "Amen," and began to participate with God to bring the fulfillment.

"For your sake, O LORD, look with favor on your desolate sanctuary… We do not make requests of you because we are righteous, but because of your great mercy. O LORD listen! O LORD, forgive! O LORD, hear and act! For your sake, O my God, do not delay" (vv. 17–19).

Daniel's prayer is a model for us as we carry before the Lord the sins of our own and former generations.

Daniel had learned to "pray the Word."

IMITATING JESUS

What better way to pray than to take the very words of Scripture and make them our own? These words continually stir me toward prayer. In reading the Gospels, I watch Jesus, knowing that His life is my example. I pray into my own life what I am observing in His. After all, it is He Who told me, "Anyone who has faith in me will do what I have been doing" (John 14:12).

> What better way to pray than to take the very words of Scripture and make them our own?

Therefore, I no longer read the Gospels simply to find what Jesus said and did, but I read them to see my own destiny. I am to become like Him! The same Spirit lives in me that lived in Him.

When I watch Jesus as He touches a leper and read that the leper was "immediately…cured of his leprosy" (Matt. 8:3), I pause, praying that kind of power to flow through me. He is the one who told me that I will do what He did.

When I *see* a woman who was "crippled by a spirit for eighteen years" (Luke 13:10), healed in one instant, I stop and ask the Lord to bring that kind of touch through me.

If Jesus could pray and see five loaves and two fish multiplied to serve thousands because there was a need (see Mark 6:30–42), why not I who have His Spirit within me?

I am no longer merely reading fascinating Bible stories, but I am being challenged to believe for more.

I pray the Word!

APOSTOLIC PRAYING

The prayers of the apostles have become my prayers. I store them inside me, waiting for a time to release them.

Some years back, when I was to officiate at a wedding, I was asked to include in the blessing over the bride and groom the words penned by Paul from a Roman jail. The prayer became so lodged within me that I have brought it out again and again. I have spoken it over others, and I have looked myself in the mirror and prophesied to me, too:

> [May God,] out of His glorious riches...strengthen you with power through his Spirit in your inner being, so that Christ [Messiah Jesus] will dwell in your hearts through faith. And I pray that you, being rooted and established in love, may have power, together with all the saints, to grasp how wide and long and high and deep is the love of Christ [Messiah Jesus], and to know this love that surpasses knowledge—that you may be filled to the measure of all the fullness of God" (Eph. 3:16–19).

Over and over again I've reached back to Scripture to grasp these prayers that have brought life to generations, and I have watched as the Spirit of God has massaged these words into other hearts:

> May the God of hope fill you with all joy and peace as you trust in Him so that you will overflow with hope by the power of the Holy Spirit (Rom. 15:13).

Overflow with hope! You have so much that you slosh out on everyone around you!

You get the point! Pray the Word!

VENTING WITH GOD

Sometimes I am encouraged, but also amused at the display of emotion expressed in biblical prayers. I almost laugh out loud every time I read the book of Numbers and come to one of Moses' outbursts, recorded in all its brashness, right there for all the world to see.

Moses had tolerated Israel's continued rebellion and grumbling as long as he could handle it. One day, after he had had all he could take, he went off to be alone with the Lord, and let go: "Why have you brought this trouble on your servant?" he cried. "What have I done to displease you that you put the burden of all these people on me? Did I conceive all these people? Did I give them birth?" he ranted. "Why do you tell me to carry them in my arms, as a nurse carries an infant, to the land you promised on oath to their forefathers?" (Num. 11:11–12).

He could have added, "I did not want to do this in the first place, remember? You are the one that insisted on my coming! I was perfectly happy in Midian with my wife and boys!"

But Moses was not finished. He had a trump up his sleeve: "I cannot carry all these people by myself; the burden is too heavy for me. If this is how you are going to treat me, put me to death right now" (vv. 14–15).

I wonder if Moses waited to see if lightning would strike, but God did not seem overly stirred by the outburst. This both encourages and challenges me to express every emotion inside me. Why not? He knows them anyway. Why hold back?

Seemingly ignoring this explosion, the Lord says to Moses: "I'll help you out. Bring me some of your key leaders and I'll take some of my Spirit I have put on you and put the Spirit on them. They'll help you. And, by the way, they keep begging for meat, so I'll give them meat—for a whole month, until it comes out their nostrils!" (This is my paraphrase. You'll have to read Numbers 11:16–20 to get the recorded version of the conversation.)

Moses had fared quite well so far and was still alive, so he continued with the eruption: "Lord, have you forgotten that there are several million of us—600,000, just counting the men? How do You propose to bring meat to that many people? If we killed all the flocks and the cattle, there would not be enough! Not even if we could empty the sea!" (Another of my paraphrases, vv. 21–22).

"Just you wait! You'll see!" the Lord answered, and Moses went on his way, perhaps still sulking. This is the man to whom the Lord had entrusted the leadership of an entire nation.

At the time, there was no hint of a reprimand from the Lord. Only later, when pride got in Moses' way and he acted like he and God together would have to produce water again, did Moses get the word that he would not be permitted to enter the Land with his people (see Num. 20:6–12).

Don't be afraid to express your feelings to the Lord. He can handle it. Use the Word as your example.

HOW LONG, O LORD?

A few years ago, I was away from home when I received some bad news about someone for whom I cared very much. It seemed that this young man had sunk deeply into drug addiction. He had been daily in my prayers, but I was seeing no effect from those prayers. One of my friends called me, and when I expressed my agony of heart, he said, "Try praying Psalm 13. That might work for you."

Don't be afraid to express your feelings to the Lord. He can handle it.

I opened my Bible to Psalm 13. Obviously I had read it before, since I have been reading the Word all my adult life. But this time it was different. It was exactly what I needed. These words became mine as I walked and poured out my lament. (I find that my legs and my brain often engage together):

> How long, O LORD? Will you forget me forever? How long will you hide your face from me? How long must I wrestle with my thoughts and every day have sorrow in my heart? How long will my enemy triumph over me? Look on me and answer, O LORD, my God (vv. 1–3).

Pretty bold talk to Almighty God, wouldn't you say? A good paraphrase might be, "Hey, Lord, remember me? Have You been listening?

Are You leaving me here high and dry? Hello, up there!"

But then in the last two verses, it's as though the psalmist catches himself and decides he'd better change his tune. Remembering God's goodness, he adds, "But...I trust in your unfailing love; my heart rejoices in your salvation...I will sing to the Lord, for He has been good to me" (vv. 5–6).

Within minutes, I had this psalm transferred to my internal hard drive. For two hours or more, I walked the streets of the quiet neighborhood near the guesthouse where I was staying. Over and over again, I prayed: "Will you forget me? How long?" And over and over again, when I came to the big word "But," my spirit lifted and I felt a fresh surge of hope.

Did praying that psalm alleviate all my concerns? No, but it put them in perspective and I had the strength to go on. *And to keep praying until the answer came.*

That's it! Keep praying until the answer comes.

One time Daniel prayed twenty-one days before *his* answer came (see Dan. 10). The Israelites prayed for hundreds of years before God sent Moses. "I have ... seen the misery of my people... I have heard them crying out... I am concerned about their suffering... I have come down to rescue them" (Ex. 3:7–8). Jesus told the story of the persistent widow in front of the judge in order to teach us to "always pray and not give up" (Luke 18:1).

'What took You so long?" we often would like to ask, but that's a question that will have to wait. His ways are always beyond our comprehension. Remind the Lord! Pray back to Him His own Word! Soak up the blessings! Store up His words.

And, in the words of both Jesus and Winston Churchill, "Never, never, never give up!"

I hope you understand the urgency. I would be happy if you are now so filled with anticipation for your future times with God that you stop reading *this* book and start reading *The Book*. Start talking to the Lord. Tell Him exactly how you feel about your situation. Don't hold back!

And remember, no matter what you are going through or will go through, He will work it all for your good if you will simply keep loving and trusting!

NOTES

1. James W. Goll, *Kneeling on the Promises* (Grand Rapids MI: Chosen Books, 1999), p. 25.
2. Young Jewish boys are called to the Torah as they enter their teen years. King Nebuchadnezzar had called for young men "from the royal family and nobility...without any physical defect, handsome, showing aptitude for every kind of learning, well informed and quick to understand" to serve in his palace (Dan. 1:3–4). Daniel had lived through five Babylonian and Persian kings from the time of his captivity to the time of his prayer for deliverance seventy years later.

CHAPTER 12

WRESTLE WITH GOD FOR THE VICTORY!

I will not let you go until you bless me.
~Genesis 32:26

Our biblical friend Jacob had an unusual wrestling match one night—a story with immense implications for a Western-style Christianity that often has difficulty persevering through adverse circumstances. All of his life, Jacob had been both the deceiver and the deceived. But in a crucial moment, he would decide whether to seize the promise God had given twenty years earlier, or to continue to be known as Jacob the Heel-Grabber, the Deceiver, the Supplanter.

When put to the test, how serious are we about our commitment to Jesus? How well do we know His promises? Do we have the spiritual energy to prevail when difficulties arise? Would we be willing to wrestle, even with God, until the answers come?

God had said to Jacob's grandfather, Abraham, "I will make you into a great nation and I will bless you" (Gen. 12:2). But Sarah was barren. Besides, she was well past childbearing age. How could the blessing come if she could not bear a child?

In her impatience and lack of faith, Sarah persuaded Abraham to "help God out" by using Sarah's maid as a surrogate mother. God was not pleased with the arrangement, insisting that the heir would come from Sarah's own womb.

At *her* age—now in her late eighties? She laughed at the ridiculous notion.

Finally, at the age of ninety, Sarah gave birth to Isaac, whose name means "Laughter." Perhaps Sarah remembered her response when the Lord told her and Abraham that she was indeed to have a son (see Gen. 18:9–15).

WAITING IN THE DARK

For some reason, the son of Abraham and Sarah's old age, Isaac, was himself forty years old before he married Rebekah (see Gen. 25:20). Rebekah was expected to conceive quickly and give birth to a son who would become the heir to all the promises God had given to Isaac's parents. But Rebekah was barren. For twenty years she waited, hoping, wondering. *Will Isaac choose another wife since I cannot give him an heir? Will I die before God delivers a son through me?*

After years of infertility, Rebekah became pregnant. But another concern soon surfaced. Something was not right with the pregnancy. When Rebekah inquired of the Lord about her unusual symptoms, He replied: "Two nations are in your womb, and two peoples from within you will be separated; one people will be stronger than the other, and the older will serve the younger" (25:23).

No doubt Rebekah told her husband about this encounter, but Isaac's later actions imply that he was not in agreement with his wife's apparent word from the Lord regarding the younger son.

When the twins were born, the first one to be delivered was red and hairy. They named him "Harry" (Esau) and nicknamed him "Red" (Edom). His brother immediately followed, holding onto Esau's heel. His parents gave this child the name "Jacob," meaning "Heel-Grabber," "Deceiver," "Supplanter," a name that defined the next years of his life.

Isaac favored Esau, the outdoorsman. Jacob was "a mama's boy" who often stayed at home with Rebekah. During those times with her, we can only assume that Jacob heard, perhaps over and over again, the story of God's revelation while the boys were in the womb. It would, therefore, have been obvious to Jacob that Esau was his father's favorite, and that there would have to be a change of heart if Jacob were ever to receive the double-inheritance blessing of a firstborn son.

OBSTACLES TO OVERCOME

The fulfillment of God's Word rarely comes without serious roadblocks. Sibling rivalry seems always to have simmered just beneath the surface in the home of Isaac and Rebekah. This rivalry forms the backdrop for two important events that would shape the family history.

The first occurred one day when Esau came home from a hunting expedition, ravenously hungry. Jacob had just prepared a nice stew, but he was not moved by brotherly love and kindness to share. Instead, he saw an opportunity to grab his brother's birthright.

"Quick, let me have some of that red stew!" Esau cried. "I'm famished!" (Gen. 25:30)

"First sell me your birthright," was Jacob's response. "Swear to me" (vv. 31, 33).

So Esau swore on oath, selling his birthright to his brother.

Score Victory # 1 for Jacob.

The second incident happened at the end of their father Isaac's life. His eyes had grown dim, his health was failing, and he knew that his time was coming to an end. Disregarding the word that Rebekah had received from the Lord, Isaac called Esau to go into the open country and bring back some wild game for a celebratory meal, after which he would give him the blessing of a firstborn son.

> The fulfillment of God's Word rarely comes without serious roadblocks.

Rebekah overheard the conversation and was not about to let this happen. Unable to trust the Lord for the fulfillment of His own promise, Rebekah took things into her own hands in much the same way that Abraham and Sarah had done in a preceding generation. She persuaded Jacob to go along with the ruse, prepared all of Isaac's favorite dishes, dressed Jacob in some of Esau's clothes that smelled of the outdoors, covered his hands and neck with goatskins, and sent him to his father.

"I am Esau your firstborn. I have done as you told me," Jacob lied, as he approached his father. "Please sit up and eat some of my game, so that you may give me your blessing" (27:19).

"How did you find it so quickly, my son?" Isaac asked, suspicious that something was askew (v. 20).

"The LORD your God gave me success," Jacob responded cautiously.

Isaac was not convinced. "Come near so I can touch you, my son, to know whether you really are my son Esau or not" (v. 21). But as the old man felt the strategically placed goatskins and caught the scent of his older son, though he was still puzzled, he was ready to bless.

"The voice is the voice of Jacob, but the hands are the hands of Esau" (v. 22), Isaac remarked as he laid his hands on his younger son and imparted the blessing: "May nations serve you and peoples bow down to you. Be lord over your brothers, and may the sons of your mother bow down to you. May those who curse you be cursed. And those who bless you be blessed" (v. 29).

Victory # 2.

No sooner had the words left Isaac's mouth than Esau returned from the field only to find that his brother, for the second time, had robbed him of his heritage. "He has deceived me these two times. He took my birthright, and now he's taken my blessing," Esau moaned (v. 36).

The animosity of the two brothers had now reached an intensity that demanded a quick solution. Esau was determined to kill his brother. When Rebekah found out about it, she urged Isaac to send Jacob back to her brother, his Uncle Laban.

Remember that we are not simply talking about Jacob and Esau. We are talking about our own lives, our God-encounters, the promises of God, and whether we have the tenacity needed to hold on until the fulfillment comes.

YOUR PILLAR OF REMEMBRANCE

The flight from Beersheba to Haran was the setting for Jacob's first encounter with the God of Grandfather Abraham and his father, Isaac. While lying on the ground under an open sky, Jacob had a dream in which angels were ascending and descending on a stairway between heaven and earth.

Above the stairway stood the Lord Himself, speaking to Jacob: "I am the LORD, the God of your father Abraham and the God of Isaac. I will give you and your descendants the land on which you are lying....All peoples on earth will be blessed through you and your offspring. I am with you...wherever you go, and I will bring you back to this land. I will not leave you until I have done what I have promised you" (28:13–15).

If Jacob had ever doubted his mother's pre-birth revelation, there was no longer a place for doubt. The promise to his grandfather, then to his father, had now passed to Jacob. Jacob carried the personalized promise from the Almighty Himself.

Jacob called the place *Bethel*, "House of God." He set up a pillar of remembrance, poured oil on the rock, and swore his own commitment to the God of his fathers: "The LORD will be my God," he swore, and following in the footsteps of his grandfather, he vowed to set aside a tenth of all his possessions for the Lord (see Gen. 28:20–22 and Gen. 14:19).

THE JACOB PAYBACK

In the midst of supernatural revelation, God-promises, and divine direction, life in the natural goes on. We may have to suffer the consequences of earlier sins and failures even at the same time we are walking toward destiny.

A few days after his amazing dream, Jacob arrived at the well in Haran and met Laban's daughter, Rachel, who would become his wife. He bargained with Laban for her hand in marriage in exchange for seven years of service, but then experienced the same kind of deceit that Jacob himself had meted out to his own father and brother. Only after the wedding did he become aware of his uncle's scheme that required an additional seven years of indentured servitude before his dowry payment for Rachel would be paid in full. For twenty years, Jacob served his dishonest father-in-law before he was ready to return to the land promised by the Lord.

"I see that your father's attitude toward me is not what it was before, but the God of my father has been with me. You know that I've worked for your father with all my strength, yet your father has cheated me by changing my wages ten times," he told his wives as they prepared for the journey home (31:5–7).

Eleven sons were born to Jacob during his years away from home, but the memory of his last encounter with Esau was still fresh. Jacob sent his wives, children, and servants ahead with lavish peace offerings for Esau–hundreds of goats, sheep, camels, and other livestock. "Your servant

Jacob is coming behind us," they were instructed to say (32:20).

With the family sent on before him, Jacob was now alone—alone with himself and his thoughts about his fractured relationship with his brother, who might still want to kill him for his trickery. Alone with the God of that former encounter twenty years earlier, the God of his father, Isaac, and his grandfather, Abraham.

HOLD ON!

Under the open skies, Jacob met the Lord a second time. A Man began to wrestle with him, but Jacob knew that this was another God-encounter. "I saw God face to face," Jacob would later testify, "and yet my life was spared" (32:30).

"Let me go for it is daybreak," the Man cried.

"I will not let you go until you bless me" (v. 21), Jacob boldly responded as he held tenaciously to the One who could assure him of the blessing.

> God was in a wrestling match with Jacob, a wrestling match in which God wanted Jacob to win!

I will not let You go until You guarantee to me that Your Word will be accomplished. Wrestle with me however You wish. I may walk with a limp for the rest of my life, but I will not let You go until I have what You promised me!

God was in a wrestling match with Jacob, a wrestling match in which God wanted Jacob to win! He wanted Jacob to lay hold of the fullness of his destiny.

"What is your name?" (v. 27) the Man (God) finally asked, in a question that would have touched Jacob to the core.

"And [in shock of realization, whispering] he said, 'Jacob' [supplanter, schemer, trickster, swindler]!" (v. 27 AMP).

And He (God) said, "Your name shall be called no more Jacob [supplanter], but Israel [contender with God]; for you have contended and have power with God and with men and have prevailed" (v. 28 AMP).

Jacob called the name of the place Peniel, meaning "face of God," saying, "For I have seen God face to face, and my life is spared and not snatched away" (v. 30 AMP).

A life-defining moment in Jacob's history! A change in his entire self-identity! He was now Israel, a name that has survived through all of history as the name through which redemption has come to earth. Israel, the Contender with God who prevailed; Israel, the God-wrestler who won; Israel, Prince of God; Israel, the man who held on until the blessing came!

GOD'S WRESTLERS

Jacob's night of wrestling is a significant story for us as we advance into the future. Declarations from the Lord that have lain dormant for centuries are ready to spring into reality. God is looking for wrestlers, those who will grapple with Him for the promise, and who refuse to give up until the assurance comes. We may have tried prematurely to usher in those promises from God, but if they are from Him, He will bring the victory. Our role is to hold on, never to let Him go.

- "All Israel will be saved!" (Rom. 11:26).

You said it Yourself, Lord. I will not let You go, Lord, until all Israel—every last one of Jacob's descendants—has a revelation of the Messiah, so that Jewish people the world over are known as Jesus-followers!

- Greater riches for the whole world when Israel comes into her fullness (see v. 12).

I may walk with a limp, but I refuse to give up until Israel and the Jewish people not only have become followers of Jesus, but have entered into their intended destiny of being a light to all the nations, until every ethnic group in the world knows about this Jewish Messiah who is the World Redeemer!

- "In that day there will be a highway from Egypt to Assyria. The Assyrians will go to Egypt and the Egyptians to Assyria. The Egyptians and Assyrians will worship together. In that day Israel will be the third, along with Egypt and Assyria [much of the Arab world today], a blessing on the earth. The LORD Almighty will bless them, saying, 'Blessed be Egypt my people, Assyria my handiwork, and Israel my inheritance'" (Isa. 19:23–25).

This is a huge promise, Lord. This has never happened, but it is written in Your Word. Arabs, Egyptians, Israelis together a blessing in the world! Wrestle me down if You will, Lord, but I have read Your Word. I know this seems impossible today. These nations are Israel's enemies. But You have given a promise, and I hold You to Your promise. One day Egyptians as well as "Assyrians" will be known as followers of Your way.

Not only God's Word for world conditions, but His word for each of us individually must be held tight if we are to walk out our own personal destiny. We may be "Jacobs," but we must become "Israels."

- "I tell you the truth, anyone who has faith in me will do what I have been doing. He will do even greater things than these, because I am going to the Father" (John 14:12).

I want to see blind eyes opening, the lame walking, the dead raised! When I read the stories of Your life, Jesus, I lean in to those miracles. You said I am supposed to do the same things! I have experienced a little, but I want more. I am holding on to Your promises. I will not let go until I have all of You!

- "If we confess our sins, he will…purify us from all unrighteousness" (1 John 1:9). "We…are being transformed into his likeness with ever-increasing glory" (2 Cor. 3:18).

It's taking a long time, Lord, but Your Word is true, and I am becoming more like You. I like me better today than when You first found me, but I want more! I want to be like You! I am only repeating what You said!

God is looking for a radical firebrand remnant of believers who are not moved by the changing world nor the growing wickedness around us. We, like Jacob, are holding on even when our spiritual hips (or our physical ones) have been put out of joint. This is not just another wrestling bout with men, or even with demons. This is a wrestling match with God...and He's pulling for us to win!

And in the meantime, if we will keep on loving Him, He will work all the wrestling for our good!

13

CALL ON JESUS!

There is no other name under heaven given to men
by which we must be saved.
~Acts 4:12

A few months ago I had the privilege of hearing Andrew White, who leads a congregation of Jesus-believers in Baghdad, Iraq. He told of a young girl in his congregation who was hospitalized and near death. The distraught father went to the clinic operated by Jesus-followers to see if they could come with him to the hospital to pray for his daughter. When they advised him that they were not authorized to go to that hospital, he consulted his pastor, Andrew White, who gave the father the following instruction:

"Call on Jesus!" Andrew told the father. "Speak His name continually as you leave here! Do not cease as you make your way back to your daughter. Stand over her and speak His Name! There is power in the Name of Jesus. Jesus! Jesus! Jesus!"

The father carefully followed the pastor's instructions. "Jesus, Jesus, Jesus!" he prayed as he left. "Jesus, Jesus, Jesus!" as he made his way back to the hospital. "Jesus, Jesus, Jesus!" he continued as he moved ever closer to his daughter's bedside. "I commit to You the life of my daughter! Jesus!"

When the father arrived at the hospital, he was greeted with the news that the hospital staff had done everything they knew to do to save his daughter, but to no avail. He was ushered into the room where her lifeless body lay under a sheet that had already been pulled over her head.

"Jesus, Jesus, Jesus!" the father continued to cry as he tenderly removed the sheet from his daughter's face.

"Daddy, I'm hungry," she said, opening her eyes and smiling into the face of her father.

Call on Jesus!

STOP! IN THE NAME OF JESUS!

A group of women gathered for a jewelry party in Florida. As they were passing around the pieces, deciding if and how much they would purchase, a gun-toting masked man entered the house, demanding the jewelry and their purses. The hostess believed in a Power greater than guns. "Stop in the Name of Jesus!" she demanded as the thief was rifling through the ladies' handbags.

Then all the women in the room began to chant the Name: "Jesus, Jesus, Jesus!"

The confused burglar dropped the purses, scattering the jewelry on the floor, and fled. Two hours later, the perplexed man was apprehended by the police, not far from the scene of his intended crime.[1]

Call on Jesus!

THE NAME THAT BREAKS DEMONIC STRONGHOLDS

About eleven o'clock one night, I received a phone call from one of our young converts. (I'll call him Carl.) He and his girlfriend (I'll call her Suzanne), later to become his wife, were driving around, recalling events and expressing their gratitude to the Lord for redeeming them from their past when, suddenly, Suzanne became catatonic. She could not speak. Her eyes were glazed. She had lost touch with reality.

That's when Carl called me to see if he could bring Suzanne to my home for prayer. He believed that together we could break the power of the enemy and restore her to sanity.

As we began to pray, the Lord gave me a picture of the battle of Ai (see Josh. 8) in which Joshua was instructed to send two separate groups of soldiers to invade enemy territory. Some would wait in ambush to descend upon the unsuspecting city from one direction. Another group would draw the men of Ai out of the city so that the battle would be approached from the opposite direction.

Carl and I were led to pray strength into the Spirit of God who resided in Suzanne, while at the same time asking for warring angels to descend upon and around Suzanne to free her from the demonic powers seeking to control her life again.

As we began to pray, I asked Suzanne to call upon the Name of Jesus deep within her. Her body was still rigid, her eyes fixed, but I knew that she had given her life to Jesus, and that He therefore lived within her.

After praying for a while, giving Suzanne time to cry out for Jesus deep within the recesses of her spirit, I asked her to bring that confession into her soul—her mind, her will, her emotions—to scream His Name inside her still listless body.

We stayed there for a while, Carl and I continuing to pray, insisting that Suzanne cry out to Jesus. "Now, Suzanne, begin to bring His Name, the Name of Jesus, across your lips," I encouraged her. "Speak His Name. Call on Jesus!"

With that, we saw her lips begin to move, ever so slightly, but this gave us hope to keep praying fervently. At last, Suzanne began to say, ever so softly, "Jesus, Jesus, Jesus..." Then louder and louder until her whole body and mind were engaged, and she was smiling at us, completely herself again.

I had an email from Carl and Suzanne recently. They are still avid followers of the One Who has redeemed them.

Call on Jesus!

***

I was just learning about all this in my early days as a pastor. One morning about 2:30, I received a phone call. "Don, would you pray for me? Jim (not his real name) just came home drunk again and, though he has never been physically abusive to me or the children, there is something different about tonight."

I hung up the phone and began to pray. I knew all about the struggles Jim was having as a war veteran and an alcoholic. I began to wonder if I should get out of bed and go to Jim's home when the second call came. "Don, could you come? I'm really afraid for my life."

I had learned enough about ministry to know that I must not go alone, so I called one of my covenant partners and asked if he would meet me and go with me.

A few minutes later, we parked and were walking toward the home, when Jim came out, appearing to be perfectly sober, and apologized for our late-night visit. We walked into the house and began to chat briefly before I laid my hand on Jim's shoulder and began to pray.

The moment I spoke the Name of Jesus, Jim became a different person—a person possessed. He lunged toward me, put his hand around my neck as if to choke me, "Don't say that, Don!" he screamed.

I have forever been grateful for those times when, just as Jesus predicted to His close friends, the Holy Spirit takes over my mouth and says things through me that I am not smart enough to have said. With adrenalin flowing and the peace of God amazingly saturating me, I said, "Jim, you can't touch me. I am covered by the blood of Jesus!"

> The moment I spoke the Name of Jesus, Jim became a different person

He sank, unconscious, at my feet. Three times that evening, the same scene occurred. Another occasion when the Lord proved to me the power of His Name!

Call on Jesus!

THE NAME THAT AWAKENS FAITH

While writing this chapter, some of us again had the rare blessing of hearing Brother Yun. As we mentioned earlier in this book, he is one of the leaders in the Chinese underground church revival.

Brother Yun's mother had come to know Jesus during the days when Western missionaries were in China. But when communism took control of the country, the missionaries were expelled, and church buildings were destroyed, his mother had no fellowship and her faith became dormant.

Meanwhile, she married and had six children. Brother Yun's older brother, age 15, died of starvation and his father was dying of cancer. His mother, despairing of life, tied a noose around her neck and was about to take her own life when she heard an audible voice: "Don't give up! Call on Jesus!"

Remembering her faith in Jesus, she awakened her five children, and told them to get up, kneel around their father's bed, and call on Jesus. Though the children had never heard this name before, and had no idea who this "Jesus" was, they obediently did as their mother said. Within the week, the father was healed, the family began to spread the news, and the mother, though illiterate and with little Bible knowledge, became the pastor of a home church. After months of praying for a Bible, the Lord delivered one to their front door. The Yun family became a part of the major awakening of faith throughout their homeland in which for years an estimated 30,000 a day are coming to believe in Jesus.

Call on Jesus!

THE NAME THAT IS ABOVE ALL NAMES

The Name of Jesus is not some mystical mantra to be pronounced for selfish gain. In fact, that could become dangerous as the sons of Sceva learned when they began to use Jesus' name without believing in Him.

"Some Jews who went around driving out evil spirits tried to invoke the name of the Lord Jesus over those who were demon-possessed. They would say, 'In the name of Jesus whom Paul preaches, I command you to come out.' Seven sons of Sceva, a Jewish chief priest, were doing this. One day, the evil spirit answered them, 'Jesus I know and Paul I know about, but who are you?' Then the man who had the evil spirit jumped on them and overpowered them all. He gave them such a beating that they ran out of the house naked and bleeding" (Acts 19:13–16).

The Name of Jesus is not some mystical mantra to be pronounced for selfish gain.

No, not a name to be chanted in some mystical sense, invoking a mysterious God, but the name of a Man who is God and who alone is our Redemption and our Strength. There are many gods, many christs, many lords, but only one Jesus of Nazareth in whom all power in heaven and earth resides.

"Why do you stare at us as if by our own power or godliness we had made this man walk?" Peter told the astonished crowd after the healing of the lame man at the Temple. "By faith in the name of Jesus, this man whom you see and know was made strong. It is Jesus' name and the faith that comes through him that has given this complete healing to him" (Acts 3:16). "It is by the name of Jesus Christ of Nazareth…that this man stands before you healed" (Acts 4:10), Peter later reported to the Sanhedrin. "There is no other name under heaven given to men by which we must be saved" (v. 12).

"God exalted him to the highest place and gave him the name that is above every name, that at the name of Jesus every knee should bow, in heaven and on earth and under the earth, and every tongue confess that Jesus Christ is Lord, to the glory of God the Father," Paul wrote the Philippians (2:9–11).

"You are to give him the name Jesus," the angel Gabriel told Miriam (Mary) when he was announcing Jesus' birth (see Luke 1:31).

His name is not God, Christ, or Lord. His name is Jesus (*Yeshua*, if you care to use the Hebrew form of His name by which his mother Miriam would have called Him).

At the conclusion of our prayer, we may add "We pray in the name of Christ," or "in Your name, O God," or "in the name of the Lord." We may know exactly of whom we are speaking, but Scripture never admonishes us to pray in God's name, in Christ's name, or in the name of the Lord, but to use the name God gave His Son—Jesus.

"I will do whatever you ask in my name," (John 14:13) are Jesus' words to His disciples. "My Father will give you whatever you ask in my name" (John 16:23). "Until now you have not asked for anything in my name…In that day you will ask in my name" (John 16:24, 26).

And Peter's message on Pentecost? "God has made this Jesus… both Lord and Christ" (Acts 2:36), therefore "Repent and be baptized…in the name of Jesus" (v.38) in order to enter into the fullness of the promises.

"Whatever you do, whether in word or deed, do it all in the name of the Lord Jesus" (Col. 3:17).

Whole worship assemblies can take place without ever speaking Jesus' Name, but it is the Name "Jesus" before whom the world will bow, the

Name of Jesus that every tongue will confess, the Name of Jesus through which miracles will come, the Name of Jesus that has been elevated above every other name.

If we would walk in His fullness and receive all that He has promised, we must learn to speak His Name, knowing assuredly that He is the One who will turn everything for our good, as we love and exalt Him.

Jesus!

NOTES

1. "Women Use Jesus' Name to Scare Away Robber," *Charisma* (March 2013), p. 20.

CHAPTER 14

KEEP IN STEP WITH THE SPIRIT!

If anyone does not have the Spirit of Christ,
he does not belong to Christ.
~Romans 8:9

    I (Don) was baptized in the Holy Spirit in 1969, the year Tod McDowell was born. I was in my 40th year. There was no physical manifestation at the time, but a faith surrender, knowing that God speaks and that my primary role is to listen for Holy Spirit prompting and to respond in obedience.

    Thirty-five years later, through the sovereign intervention of Holy Spirit, God's call through a prophet, His confirming voice to me, then to Tod, his wife Rachel, and their family, Tod and I began listening and walking together. This ultimately led to the McDowells' move to Nashville where we have been in almost daily communication under the umbrella of the Holy Spirit's beckoning. Not only Tod and Rachel, but also their children, Mandy, Micah, Makai'o and Moses, listen together for instructions from God regarding ministry, travel, and life.

    What I have written in the rest of the book is impacted by our lives together. Even though up until now, I have more often been the scribe, this book would not have happened had it not been for the revelation we have received together. What better place to hear from Tod directly than to learn how he came to follow Jesus and how he "keeps in step with the Spirit."

~TOD MCDOWELL~

Young Samuel learned to hear the voice of the Lord early in childhood while serving the prophet Eli and sleeping near the Ark of the Covenant. The Lord called to Samuel, but since he had never heard God's voice, Samuel assumed that Eli was calling.

"Here I am," Samuel said as he ran to Eli's side. "Here I am; you called me" (1 Sam 3:5).

You probably know the rest of the story. This happened three times, before Eli realized that God was calling Samuel, that "the word of the LORD had not yet been revealed to him" (v. 7). In other words, Samuel had not learned to recognize God's voice.

"Go and lie down," Eli told Samuel, "If he calls you say, 'Speak, LORD, for your servant is listening'" (v. 9).

Samuel returned to his place, ready to listen for God's voice.

EARLY HOLY SPIRIT ENCOUNTER

I had my own first encounter with the Lord at a time when I did not recognize who was at work.

In my early years, our family was broken up through my parents' divorce. They did the best they could with the malfunctioning examples they had, but much of my early years I spent alone, walking through the woods and stealing candy from stores for pleasure. Nights were dreaded because of the monster-like demons that filled my dreams and the grotesque images that left me paralyzed with fear. I would awaken in panic and eventually cry myself back to sleep, only to awaken again with the same horrific scenes. This happened again and again until one night, through nothing unusual that I had done, the Lord showed up and pierced my darkness. I knew nothing about God and His ways, and not until years later was I able to identify this early God-visit as a preparation for me to meet Jesus and begin to be led by His Spirit.

In the middle of one of my nightly terrors, with darkness engulfing me and horrendous creatures choking me, I felt my life slipping away. Suddenly the screen of my eight-year-old mind became bright white, brilliant white, like staring into the sun. Darkness fled. Fear was gone and there were no more demonic creatures. Something or Someone had come to save me and pull me out of the abyss. In the next moment in my dream/vision, I was sitting on a swing in my favorite park—peaceful, sunny, and laughing in total freedom and perfect joy. I awoke with a sense that my life had been handed back to me. I had no idea who had so helped me, but never again did the demonic creatures return.

One year later, through the invitation of a school friend, I walked into a small church that met in the recreation building about one hundred yards from the swing in the park of my dream. I gave my life to Jesus, was baptized in the creek about thirty yards from the swing, and never turned back, even though no one in my immediate family at that time was following Jesus.

While attending a youth camp nine years later, I learned more about the work and gifts of the Holy Spirit. Hungry for more, I went up for prayer for God's Holy Spirit to be released in and through me. The only way I know how to describe the difference is that I felt I advanced from a spiritual bike ride to a drive in a high-powered car.

I was experiencing what Jesus told His disciples after His resurrection and before His ascension: "You will receive power when the Holy Spirit comes on you" (Acts 1:8), what the disciples experienced a few days later when they were "filled with the Holy Spirit and began to speak in other tongues as the Spirit enabled them" (2:4). Life has not always been a blaze of glory since that day, but I have never been the same. I am filled with an inexpressible joy of God that transcends every hardship and keeps me surrendered to His fullness in my life.

From that day forward, the Power present in my childhood encounter, the Power who now has a name—Jesus—has my life. His Spirit is my Counselor, my Encourager, the One who convicts me of sin, who leads me in righteousness (see John 16:8–11), my Strength, Encourager and my Comforter (see 1 Corinthians 14:3). "His incomparably great power… like the working of his mighty strength, which he exerted in Christ when he raised him from the dead" (Eph. 1:19–20) is within me.

PASSING THE TEST

Like Samuel's nighttime encounter with God when he was learning to listen to His voice, the listening sometimes has its challenging side. In Samuel's encounter, God told him about the judgment that was to come to his mentor Eli. This was not what Samuel expected or wanted to hear, but was a test as to whether he would be faithful to carry out God's revelation and His instructions, even when they were not his choice at all.

I've had some of those tests. You will, too, as you follow closely the voice of the Spirit.

One of my difficult encounters happened during my courtship days with Rachel. We both knew Jesus and were walking forward together, always wanting to know His will. Most of our courtship took place in worship assemblies, in hospitals and nursing homes, or in ministry to the poor. After seeing each other for several months, I sensed Holy Spirit taking our relationship to another level, and even felt that our next time together was to be a special time of revelation for us.

I was full of expectation when I picked her up and headed for our special spot on the edge of some cliffs overlooking a bay on the coast. As we drove to our destination, I kept asking Holy Spirit what gift was He to give us? Why was this night to be so special? But God is not on our timing, so I had to be patient.

As we walked up the steep bank to our private piece of land, my mind was racing. When we found our spot, we were surprised to find a freshly lit fire with wood burning, yet no one in sight. We looked around, but it was as though some special angel had built us a fire and left just in time for us to have the full enjoyment. I was in awe, basking in the tangible sense of the Lord's presence with my arm around the most beautiful woman I had ever met.

I began again to ask the Lord, *What is going to be so special? Is this the night of our first kiss? What are You revealing?*

At last there was an answer: *Don't kiss until your wedding day, and don't hold hands with fingers interlocking until you are engaged.*

I was undone! The Voice was the Voice of God, but the instructions were devastating. My first response was to rebuke the enemy. He wants to steal the joy of this moment, I thought. Surely I had heard wrong.

I'll ask again.

Don't kiss until marriage, and don't hold hands with fingers interlocking until you are engaged.

I was silent, allowing time for God to rearrange my heart. *Maybe this is just a test, and once I agree to be obedient, He will release me. Surely I have heard wrong.*

But the same phrase kept repeating inside me.

Finally in a moment of resignation and surrender, I hesitatingly said to Rachel, "What would you think if we didn't kiss until marriage and if we didn't hold hands until we were engaged?"

I expected her to laugh, but her response was immediate, "I think that's right."

I was still in a state of shock, but after a short pause, I was able to look up to the heavens and say, "*This is the next level in our relationship, isn't it?*"

Yes, He said, and my heart was sealed.

"Whether you turn to the right or to the left, your ears will hear a voice behind you, saying, 'This is the way; walk in it," Isaiah said, centuries before Jesus came (30:21). "He who belongs to God hears what God says" (John 8:47), Jesus affirmed. "My sheep listen to my voice" (10:27).

I am not asking you to follow God's instructions for Rachel and me, but if we were going to be obedient to this God whom we knew to be the only true God and to the instructions of His Holy Spirit, if we were to experience the fullness of His joy for us, our path was now clear.

Two years and seven months later, after being separated through ministry much of the time, we kissed for the first time in front of three hundred of our closest friends and family as we sealed a life covenant together in marriage. God has been faithful to His covenant. Over twenty years of marriage and four children later, He has continued to pursue us, talk to us, change us and bless us.

LIKE THE WIND

One night, Jesus was talking to Nicodemus about the work of God's Spirit. He told Nicodemus that he needed to be born again. Nicodemus had no idea what Jesus meant. "How can a man be born when he is old?" he asked (John 3:4).

Jesus responded to Nicodemus by comparing natural birth and spiritual birth. "Spirit gives birth to spirit" (v. 6), Jesus said, then proceeded to compare Holy Spirit's work to the wind. "The wind blows wherever it pleases. You hear the sound but you cannot tell where it comes from or where it is going. So it is with everyone born of the Spirit" (v. 8)

We sometimes overlook the fact that Jesus is not only saying that Holy Spirit is like the wind, which He is, but that "everyone born of the Spirit" is like the wind. We must keep our spiritual sails hoisted in order to be sure that we are moving in the direction God has intended. Sometimes that changes as the Wind redirects us.

> "Everyone born of the Spirit" is like the wind.

Rachel and I have had a few of those experiences as well. Up until the year 2005, after having served for fifteen years in Youth with A Mission's Kona, Hawaii base, we began to assume this would be our launching place for the rest of our lives. Our four children were born in Kona. We had traveled to many nations on outreaches. I had served on the President's Council with YWAM founders and base leaders, Loren and Darlene Cunningham. I had led in schools and taught in the Biblical Studies program of the University of the Nations. We had our first home. And besides all this, we were a family of surfers living on an island paradise with incredible surf!

But remember that we are like the wind. We never know where the gale force of Holy Spirit is going to take us.

Even though our lives were full, I began to sense that there was more. I began to ask the Lord why there was still uneasiness within me. What were the keys to this world revival for which we were all yearning?

So I withdrew from all ministry for forty days so that I could give myself to prayer and fasting, seeking the Lord for greater clarity. I asked my staff to hold any calls unless they were essential, so that I could spend hours each day in worship and prayer.

On day 35 of the fast was the day I met Don. As he began sharing with me and praying for me, Holy Spirit wind started a fresh breeze. With his call from Israel one month later the wind velocity increased, but none of us at that time could have imagined that the wind would land us in

Nashville two years later, and that I would become the Director of the ministry Don founded.

But remember, "the wind blows wherever it pleases. You hear its sound, but you cannot tell where it comes from or where it is going."

Exciting life in Jesus! Never boring! Sometimes momentarily excruciating, but never boring!

HOLY SPIRIT CONVICTION

One of the roles of Holy Spirit in our lives is to "convict... of guilt in regard to sin and righteousness and judgment" (John 16:8), so that we can confess those sins and enter into greater purity and wholeness (see 1 John 1:9).

Soon after we moved from Kona to Nashville, I became convicted that I needed to let Don know of one of the sin patterns that continued to ensnare me. I never will forget the day I felt the time had come for me to broach the subject. Don and I shared an office, with desks across the room from each other. I stopped what I was doing, turned my chair toward him, held on to the sides of the chair, and began, "I need to confess something to you."

The room stopped. This was a huge risk for me. I had just moved our family of six to Tennessee to work with Don, and now I was not sure he would want to continue working with me.

Carefully choosing my words, I talked to him about some of the failures that kept tripping me up. When I was finished, Don got up, came over to me, knelt down, embraced me, and began to speak a prayer of forgiveness and victory, pulling on heaven in a way that gave me a cleansed conscience and renewed hope. Strangely enough, he will tell you that his love and appreciation for me became even stronger that day because I had emptied myself before him, sharing my deepest needs. My life has not been flawless since that day, but I have had victories that I had never before experienced.

But confession of this sort is rarely one way. I had learned to trust Don because of his unusual life transparency, grateful for a father figure with whom I could be crassly honest.

Not long after that office encounter, I received a call from Don. "I have to see you before the day is over," he said. "There is something I need to confess to you – a pattern that has continually tripped me, and I want it broken." You have to realize that this man is no longer a teenager (he says he is in double overtime; he's past 80), but he is still determined to grow up into the image of Jesus. Perhaps he could have become victorious without his confession to me, but this kind of one-another-ness has enhanced our ability to walk together. We keep clean slates with each other and with others, are quick to confess and quick to forgive. Don has helped me to become a better husband to Rachel and father to my children, never putting ministry above family.

Holy Spirit is an excellent "Convict-er." He may use people, an evangelist, a teacher, a pastor, but without Holy Spirit's work, there is no conviction of sin. I may not like the moment of conviction, but I love what God is making of me as I cooperate with Him.

Two voices vie for our attention.

TWO VOICES

One of the factors that helps us move into greater wholeness of life is not only discerning the voice of Holy Spirit and responding, but also learning to distinguish between the two external voices that vie for our attention—the voice of God and the voice of the enemy.

I love what I consider the illustrative interaction between Jesus and Peter when Jesus was teaching Peter how to detect those two voices.

"Who do people say the Son of Man is?" Jesus asked his disciples, then added, "What about you? Who do you say I am?" (Matt. 16:15).

Peter, so often the first one to speak up, had a quick response: "You are the [Messiah], the Son of the living God" (v. 16).

Here is where the humor begins. Jesus must have looked directly into Peter's eyes and, among other things, said, "This was not revealed to you by man, but by my Father in heaven" (v. 17).

I always imagine the surprise written across Peter's face. Since he was always so quick to speak, I can imagine his looking back at Jesus and saying, "What do you mean? God revealed that to me? I thought I thought of it myself," to which Jesus might have responded, "No, Peter, that was revelation. You did not think of that by yourself. God revealed it. That's the way Father speaks. Pay attention. Sometimes it may seem to be your own thoughts, but some things are beyond your own natural comprehension or ability."

Perhaps still a bit perplexed, Peter walked on.

In a little while, Jesus began to talk to the disciples about His eminent death. Peter listened in disbelief, then "took [Jesus] aside and began to rebuke him. 'Never, Lord! This shall never happen to you!'" (v. 22).

Imagine the scene! After all those years of walking with Jesus, and just having confirmed that Jesus is truly the Son of God, the Messiah, Peter pulls Him aside to rebuke Him.

"Get behind me, Satan!" Jesus responds as He gazes into Peter's eyes again. "You are a stumbling block to me; you do not have in mind the things of God, but the things of men'" (v. 23).

Peter must have been totally puzzled by now. Only a few moments ago, Jesus had told him that he was speaking God's revelation, and now, looking straight at him, Jesus seems to be calling Peter "Satan."

"Lord, you were looking at me when you said that!" Peter may have wanted to respond, to which Jesus could have said, "That's right, Peter. Pay close attention. You heard from the Father earlier, but now the voice is that of the enemy. Learn to tell the difference."

Because of my early childhood trauma and my exposure to things that should never have been in a child's life, I sometimes had an unholy curiosity and would receive temptations for which I would accuse myself. But understanding Jesus' encounter with Peter that day helped me to understand that the enemy would put thoughts into my own head, then turn around and accuse me of thinking them. This Jesus-Peter story taught me to turn those thoughts back in the face of the enemy and not to accept them as thoughts that had come from my own God-surrendered heart.

> Our primary role in life is to listen to the Spirit and respond in obedience.

Our primary role in life is to listen to the Spirit and respond in obedience. As we move into the future that will contain the world's greatest wickedness as well as the world's greatest righteousness, it is essential that we are open to the fullness of Holy Spirit.

He will always guide into truth (see John 16:12–13), never in contradiction to the revealed Word given us in Scripture, and He will always come in gentleness.

When He descended on Jesus at His baptism, He came "like a dove" (Luke 3:22). This is significant! He did not come like a hawk or an eagle, but a dove. A dove is a non-aggressive, gentle bird. I've interacted with them many times while living in Hawaii. Gentleness and calm attracts them. Busy-ness and activity repels them. We must often halt our much activity to attract Holy Spirit. Then we will enter into the grandest outpouring of Holy Spirit in history.

"I will pour out my Spirit on all people," is Joel's prophecy (2:28). "I will put my Spirit in you and move you to follow my decrees and be careful to keep my laws," Ezekiel affirmed (36:27). "Streams of living water will flow from within you" (John 7:39), Jesus promised. You will "shine like stars in the universe as you hold out the word of life" (Phil. 2:15), Paul proclaimed.

Good days are ahead! Hold on! Don't give up! Put up your sails! Feel the wind of the Spirit! Be blown by that wind! Everything is working for our good!

15

LIVE IN COMMUNITY!

Be devoted to one another in brotherly love.
~Romans 12:10

The two scenes are still very vivid in my memory – two families, two completely different scenarios. One is the sight of dozens, even hundreds, crowding into a hospital chapel for prayer, lingering in the hallways outside the room of a young mother and wife whose life was hanging in the balance. The other is the picture of a vacant parking lot, an empty funeral home, and a couple standing alone in front of an open casket.

The first scene followed a tragic accident. A mother was hovering between life and death in intensive care. The waiting room, chapel, and parking lots were filled to capacity with praying, warring, loving friends, young and old. Those present had frequented each other's homes and visited together in prayer meetings, Bible studies, and soccer games. Birthday celebrations and weddings, baby showers, and vacations were common occasions. They loved each other with a devotion reserved for the followers of Jesus. Not all were in the same room on Sunday morning, but they lived in community.

The second scene was a funeral home. The father of one of the couples who regularly attended our congregation had died, and I was not sure how many people even knew about it. I wanted to be present, partially because I was concerned that the couple, though reasonably well-known and long-time residents in the city and members of the "church," stayed pretty much to themselves. They were not quick to share life with others. Their home was generally devoid of friends. Birthdays and vacations were taken alone, if they were celebrated at all.

I drove to the funeral home and found that indeed the parking lot was empty. I walked in to find the couple alone beside the casket in the corner of the room. There were no friends present. This couple was consistently present at the Sunday morning gatherings, but they did not live in community. Sitting in a pew, singing together, and listening to the messages week after week does not produce community.

"CHURCH" IS TOGETHERNESS

"Church" is an unfortunate mistranslation of the Greek word *ekklesia*—literally meaning "called out." The Greek word carries no connotation of a building, but of people.

William Tyndale understood this. In his 1525 completed text of the New Testament, there is no "church." There is only "community." Even under great pressure to translate *ekklesia* as "church," Tyndale resisted and translated with the best word he could find in the English language for the translation of *ekklesia*—"community."[1]

> "Church" is an unfortunate mistranslation of the Greek word *ekklesia*—literally meaning "called out."

Martin Luther had the same problem. As he was defying the Church in translating Scripture, using the original texts as nearly as he could do so, he refused the German word *Kirche* (church) in favor of the word *Gemeinde* (community) for translating *ekklesia*. There is no "church" in Luther's German Bible. Luther understood that "community" is different from "church."[2]

Under the oversight of King James of England almost a century later, the translators forsook Tyndale's definition and used the word that more aptly described the conditions of the early seventeenth-century Church of England. After all, King James was the official head of the Church of England, and the Church of England knew only cathedrals and buildings as the center for Christians.[3]

Daniel Gruber was attempting to drive this point home in his book, *The Separation of Church & Faith*, in the chapter entitled "A Good Church is Hard to Find." He shockingly but accurately stated, "There is no 'church' in the biblical text. The 'Church' is not the biblical *ekklesia*. Every time you see the word 'church' in a Bible, you are seeing a place where the translators did not translate the text, but distorted it instead, for the sake of tradition. Often it is done without thinking about it, simply because the hold of Christian tradition is so strong.....'[4]

"Whatever the case may be, 'assembly,' 'congregation,' and 'community' are adequate translations of *ekklesia* in the biblical context, 'Church' is not a translation. It is an invention that replaces proper translation. It gives a meaning which is not contained in *ekklesia*. It conveys a concept that is not in the Scriptures."[5] You may have to work with this one for a while, but Gruber even crassly suggests, "There is no such thing as a church age since there is no such thing as a church."[6]

Jesus came to redeem a people separated to Himself, a people who live in community with each other and love each other with a love that only God can produce and which serves to draw others into the kingdom. The biblical record tells us that in the middle of the persecution of those early days, "more and more men and women believed in the Lord and were added to their number" (Acts 5:14).

Tyndale and Luther both knew that the New Covenant emphasis was not gatherings in specially constructed buildings, since church buildings did not make their appearance until the 3rd or early 4th century. They knew that the *ekklesia* is the body of people who are committed to the God of Abraham, Isaac and Jacob, and to His Promised Messiah who has been revealed to us through the Holy Spirit.

We may object to this distinction being made regarding the translation of *ekklesia*, and we may insist that we have never intended to imply that the "church" is a building. However, a very large percentage of those who understand the difference and who vigorously defend the "church" as the people, still refer to buildings as "churches": "We were on our way to the church (meaning a building)", or, pointing to a building, "That's the so-and-so Church."

EARLY BELIEVERS MET IN HOMES

Believers, in the early centuries after Jesus, did not have this problem as it relates to fine buildings. Nor do the people of God in the persecuted areas of the world today.

"They broke bread in their homes," Luke tells us (Acts 2:46). When Saul was looking for believers in Jesus, he did not try to find meetings in church buildings. There were none. He went "from house to house (where he) dragged men and women and put them in prison" (8:3).

Peter, after being miraculously released from prison, went to a place he must have known was a favorite gathering place for believers. Indeed, He found an all-night prayer meeting in the home of John Mark's mother, Mary (see Acts 12:12–14).

Paul continually sent greetings to the community of believers. "Greet Priscilla and Aquila (and) the church that meets at their house" (Rom. 16:3; see also 1 Corinthians 16:19). "Give my greetings ... to Nympha and the church in her house" (Col. 4:15). "To Archippus our fellow soldier and to the church that meets in your home" (Philem. 1–2).

We in the West often have some of the finest homes in the world, yet we build superstructures as the meeting places for believers, rather than using our homes as was done in the early centuries.

Even in our day, in the areas of the world where the gospel of Jesus is advancing most rapidly, often there are no buildings and no paid clergy. More often, the people of God are being harassed, arrested, imprisoned, and even killed for their faith. Believers gather in small assemblies, sometimes even mouthing hymns so as not to awaken the curiosity of neighbors who could call the police.

In my office, there is a framed, cherished picture of a communion service in a forest, an open-air assembly being secretly held during the reign of communism in Eastern Europe. A brother who lived through that era in Eastern Europe informed us that at times no notification of any kind went out to tell where the congregation would meet the next time, lest the message be intercepted by the secret police and some or all would be arrested and imprisoned. Each member had to listen to Holy Spirit's directions in order to find the next meeting place.

Many of us are aware that we in the West may one day find ourselves in similar circumstances. We may be forced into real community before the return of Jesus. This happened when communism began its reign in China. Church buildings were destroyed. Leaders were dispersed and often killed. If such a situation should come to the West, we may learn who are the true disciples of Jesus and who are simply culturally Christian.

RESTORING COMMUNITY

All of this reminds me of one of the significant times in the life of Jesus when He was continually barraged with questions. More often than not, he did not directly answer the questions, often replying with another question. On one occasion, this was not the case.

A group of Pharisees had observed Jesus for days and they were eager to find a question that would trip Him up so that His answer could be used against Him. Knowing that all of God's commandments are important, one of the Pharisees came up with a trick question: "Teacher, which is the greatest commandment in the Law?" (Matt. 22:36).

In other words, "We all know that there are 613 commandments, and surely you know that they are all of equal importance, so how are you going to respond to this one? What do you think? Which one is most important?"

Without hesitation, Jesus replied, "The most important one is this: 'Hear, O Israel, the Lord our God the Lord is one. Love the Lord your God with all your heart and with all your soul and with all your mind and with all your strength.' The second is this: 'Love your neighbor as yourself.' There is no commandment greater than these" (Mark 12:29–31). "All the law and the prophets hang on these two commandments" (Matt. 22:40).

The Pharisee who asked the question was so surprised by Jesus' reply that, before he had time to think, he blurted out, in front of his fellow-Pharisees, "Well said, teacher. You are right in saying that God is one and there is no other but him. To love him with all your heart, with all your understanding and with all your strength, and to love your neighbor as yourself is more important than all burnt offerings and sacrifices" (Mark 12:32–33).

In other words, "I would never have thought of it this way, but of course if we love God with all our hearts, and if we love our neighbors as ourselves, then we will obey all of God's laws. We will have no other gods, we will not make idols, we will not take His name in vain, we will honor His holy day, and we will treat others well, honoring our parents, never murdering, stealing, lying, or coveting" (see Ex. 20:1–17, author's paraphrase).

Jesus' answer to the Pharisee was a call to keep God in proper priority and to live in community with each other. His was not a call to build elaborate cathedrals in His honor, nor to spend billions of dollars having the finest all-purpose campuses in the world. He did not call us to once-a-week meetings in those houses. He did not have in mind that we would sit for hours listening to a man or woman bring a nice, even challenging message. He was not even primarily interested in our production of the most awesome worship music the world has ever known. Some of these things may come as an outworking of our love for God and for each other, but if we replace the first and second commandments with anything, including any of the above, we have digressed from the very reason Jesus came – to restore us to God the Father and to restore us to each other.

> We can live all our lives in "church" and never know "community," never know *ekklesia*.

I am grieved each time I hear of another pastor or television personality who has had a moral failure, but I am also convinced that, though these men or women may have been in "church" all of their lives, many of them have never lived in "community." I would dare also to say that disciples of Jesus who live in God-intended "community" will not experience moral or ethical failure. Why? Because they are accountable to others who live close to them and help them to stay aware of dangers.

We can live all our lives in "church" and never know "community," never know *ekklesia*.

LOVE GOD, LOVE ONE ANOTHER

We see this example of loving God and loving each other continuing in the lives of the early apostles and disciples. Paul and the other writers of Scripture often break wide open in praise to God before they even state the reason for their letter-writing:

"Praise be to the God and Father of our Lord Jesus Christ" (2 Cor. 1:3).

"Grace and peace to you from God the Father and the Lord Jesus Christ, who gave himself for our sins to rescue us from the present evil age, according to the will of our God and Father, to whom be glory forever and ever. Amen" (Gal. 1:3–5).

"Praise be to the God and Father of our Lord Jesus Christ, who has blessed us in the heavenly realms with every spiritual blessing in Christ" (Eph. 1:3).

"[Jesus] is the image of the invisible God, the firstborn over all creation. For by him all things were created, things in heaven and on earth, visible and invisible, whether thrones or powers or rulers or authorities, all things were created by him and for him. He is before all things, and in him all things hold together" (Col. 1:15–17).

"Praise be to the God and Father of our Lord Jesus Christ! In his great mercy he has given us new birth into a living hope through the resurrection of Jesus Christ from the dead, and into an inheritance that can never perish, spoil or fade" (1 Pet. 1:3–4).

"His divine power has given us everything we need for life and godliness" (2 Pet. 1:3).

These men had their priorities established. First priority, first commandment: Love God!

In the same way, apostolic writings are filled with the challenge lovingly to relate to each other.

Second priority, second commandment: Love each other:

"Dear friends, let us love one another, for love comes from God. Everyone who loves has been born of God and knows God... since God so loved us, we also ought to love one another... If anyone says, 'I love God,' yet hates his brother, he is a liar. For anyone who does not love his brother, whom he has seen, cannot love God, whom he has not seen" (1 John 4:7–20).

"Be devoted to one another in brotherly love. Honor one another above yourselves....Share with God's people who are in need. Practice hospitality....Rejoice with those who rejoice; mourn with those who mourn. Live in harmony with one another" (Rom. 12:10–16).

"Accept one another, then, just as Christ accepted you, in order to bring praise to God" (15:7).

"Encourage one another" (2 Cor. 13:11).

"As we have opportunity, let us do good to all people, especially to those who belong to the family of believers" (Gal. 6:10).

"Be completely humble and gentle; be patient, bearing with one another in love" (Eph. 4:2).

"Greet one another with a holy kiss" (Rom. 16:16).

"Greet one another with a holy kiss" (1 Cor. 16:20).

"Greet one another with a holy kiss" (2 Cor. 13:12).

Keep the priorities! Love each other! Live in one-another-ness! Live in community! Be sure that "church" does not push out "community." If you are not walking with a few close friends in the kingdom, friends who will challenge you to live closer to God, friends to whom you confess sins and ask for prayer, friends who confess their sins and their needs to you and receive your prayer, if you are not *walking in the light* with a few close friends, then you may have been in church all your life, may even be on the front row of the larger assemblies every week, but you are not living in that to which Jesus has called us.

As we learn to move forward with a priority of loving God and loving each other in tangible and life-transforming ways, we will enter more completely into that confidence and joy reserved for Jesus-followers, because we know that in the end, everything is working for our good. That is His promise! Never forget!

NOTES

1. Daniel Gruber, *The Separation of Church & Faith, Vol. One Copernicus and the Jews* (Hanover, NH: Elijah Publishing, 2005), p. 65.
2. Ibid. (and my own fluency in the German language)
3. Ibid., p. 66.
4. Ibid., p. 67.
5. Ibid., p. 65.
6. Ibid., p. 67.

CHAPTER 16

FINISH WELL!

I have fought the good fight, I have finished the race, I have kept the faith,
~2 Timothy 4:7

There are portions of Scripture that I dread reading. I know what's coming. I have read them before, and I don't want to read them again. One of those Scriptures is 1 Kings 11:1–6, a description of the closing days of King Solomon's life.

Solomon had an auspicious beginning. God appeared to him shortly after he ascended the throne of Israel and instructed Solomon to ask for "whatever you want me to give you" (1 Kings 3:5).

Solomon's reply is a model of humility: "I am only a little child, and do not know how to carry out my duties....So give your servant a discerning heart to govern your people and to distinguish between right and wrong" (vv. 7–9).

God's answer? "Since you have asked for this and not for long life or wealth for yourself, nor have you asked for the death of your enemies but for discernment in administering justice, I will do what you have asked, I will give you a wise and discerning heart, so that there will never have been anyone like you, nor will there ever be. Moreover, I will give you what you have not asked for – both riches and honor" (vv. 10–13).

Fast forward seven chapters—past the wise ruling regarding the two prostitutes who were claiming the same child as their son, past the visit of the Queen of Sheba, past the building of the Temple, past bringing the Ark of the Covenant into the Temple and properly placing it in the Holy of Holies, past the cloud of God's Presence so thick that "the priests could not perform their service because of the cloud, for the glory of the LORD filled his temple"(8:10), past Solomon's humble prayer dedicating the Temple and God's response to him, promising him that his prayer had been heard and that God's own "eyes and heart" would "always be there" (9:3)—past all this. Then move over to 1 Kings 11 and prepare for your heart to sink as you read:

"King Solomon, however, loved many foreign women...his wives turned his heart after other gods... So Solomon did evil in the eyes of the LORD; he did not follow the LORD completely as David his father had done" (vv. 1–6).

What happened?

Lust was clearly his downfall, but there seem to have been a number of compromises before those at the close of his life.

WORDS OF WARNING!

Moses warned about the very things that tripped up Solomon. Listen to Moses' admonition:

"When you enter the land the LORD your God is giving you and have taken possession of it and settled in it, and you say, 'Let us set a king over us like all the nations around us....' When he takes the throne of his kingdom, he is to write for himself on a scroll a copy of this law, taken from that of the priests, who are Levites. It is to be with him, and he is to read it all the days of his life so that he may learn to revere the LORD his God and follow carefully all the words of this law and these decrees, and not consider himself better than his brothers and turn from the law to the right or to the left" (Deut. 17:14–20).

Solomon was to "read [the scroll] all the days of his life." He was to "follow carefully all the words" of God's laws and decrees. He was not to "consider himself better than his brothers."

But Solomon became distracted through the very blessings God gave him. If only Solomon had listened to Moses! His warnings were very precise:

- "The king...must not acquire great numbers of horses for himself or make the people return to Egypt to get more of them" (Deut. 17:16), God had said.

  But Solomon was not reading the scrolls!

  "Solomon accumulated chariots and horses; he had fourteen hundred chariots and twelve thousand horses....Solomon's horses were imported from Egypt....[He] imported a chariot from Egypt for six hundred shekels of silver and a horse for a hundred and fifty" (1 Kings 10:26, 28–29).

- The king was not to "accumulate large amounts of silver and gold" (Deut. 17:17), was God's warning

  But...

  "The weight of the gold that Solomon received yearly was 666 talents, not including the revenues from merchants and traders and from all the Arabian kings and the governors of the land. King Solomon made two hundred shields of hammered gold; six hundred bekas of gold went into each shield. He also made three small shields of hammered gold, with three minas of gold in each shield....Then the king made a great throne inlaid with ivory and overlaid with fine gold....All King Solomon's goblets were gold, and all the household articles in the Palace of the Forest of Lebanon were pure gold....Once every three years [a fleet of trading ships] returned, carrying gold, silver.... The king made silver as common in Jerusalem as stones" (1 Kings 10:14–18, 21–22, 27).

- "The king "must not take many wives, or his heart will be led astray" (Deut. 17:17).

  But...

  "[Solomon] had seven hundred wives of royal birth and three hundred concubines, and his wives led him astray. As Solomon grew old, his wives turned his heart after other gods, and his heart was not fully devoted to the LORD his God....He followed Ashtoreth, the goddess of the Sidonians, and Molech the detestable god of the Ammonites. So Solomon did evil in the eyes of the Lord.... On a hill east of Jerusalem, Solomon built a high place for Chemosh the detestable god of Moab, and for Molech the detestable god of the Ammonites. He did the same for all his foreign wives, who burned incense and offered sacrifices to their gods" (1 Kings 11:3–8).

Solomon followed Ashtoreth and Molech? In case you happen not to remember, Molech was worshipped through child sacrifice; Ashtoreth, through the most perverse forms of sexual immorality.

Solomon started out so strong, so humble—with a wisdom that was unsurpassed. He ended his life as an evil, depraved idolater.

"The Lord became angry with Solomon because his heart had turned away from the Lord, the God of Israel, who had appeared to him twice" (v. 9).

OTHERS WHO DID NOT FINISH WELL

The biblical accounts of God's principal characters give us repeated examples and warnings of once faithful God-followers who didn't finish well.

Solomon's son, Rehoboam, was a rebel. Grandson Abijah was even worse. "He committed all the sins his father had done before him; his heart was not fully devoted to the Lord his God, as the heart of David his forefather had been" (1 Kings 15:3).

Asa, Solomon's great-grandson, was different. He had a remarkable Godly beginning. He "did what was right in the eyes of the Lord, as his father David had done. He expelled the male shrine prostitutes from the land and got rid of all the idols his fathers had made....He even deposed his grandmother...because she had made a repulsive Asherah pole" (vv. 11–13). High places were removed. When a foreign army marched out against Judah, Asa turned to the Lord in prayer, and was saved from his enemy.

> Solomon started out so strong, so humble—with a wisdom that was unsurpassed.

But in the thirty-sixth year of Asa's reign, something happened. The king of Israel marched out against him, and Asa turned to neighboring

Syria for help rather than calling on the Lord. Hanani, the prophet, confronted him. Asa was unrepentant and angry. He had Hanani thrown into prison. Three years later, Asa "was afflicted with a disease in his feet. Though his disease was severe, even in his illness, he did not seek help from the LORD, but only from the physicians" (2 Chron. 16:12). A year later he was dead.

Asa did not finish well.

ON GUARD!

Lust—greed—pride—lurking near all of us. "Be on your guard" (1 Cor. 16:13; 2 Pet. 3:17), warn both Paul and Peter. "If you think you are standing firm, be careful that you don't fall!" (1 Cor. 10:12).

I've seen too many men and women who started strong, but stumbled severely before the finish line. I remember well the days of the Jesus Movement in the late 60s and early 70s. I can still see some of those passionate new disciples who were baptized in swimming pools, bathtubs, and rivers. I've lain on the floor with them, praying until the early morning hours. I've sat for hours in their dorm rooms, in parks and coffee shops. I've looked into their eyes and seen the yearning for the fullness of God and watched as they drank in the Holy Spirit with which they overcame the most debilitating of drug and alcohol addictions, sexual cravings, and other godless dysfunctions. I've listened to the songs that were born of their passionate faith.

> I've seen too many men and women who started strong, but stumbled severely before the finish line.

I am grateful still to be walking with many of those who have never lost the fire. They are more zealous for the things of God today than in those early Jesus Movement days. They are yearning for more and are being used of God all over the world.

But I have also watched as, through the years, the fervor of many has grown cold. Some have returned, as Peter would say, to their own "vomit," like "a sow that is washed goes back to her wallowing in the mud" (2 Pet. 2:22). They are following the example of Solomon and his sons who, in surrendering to their own lust, greed, and pride, have forsaken the King.

I also grieve over public figures - television evangelists, pastors of great churches, and others - who seemed to walk with great passion for Jesus, but were found later to have lived lives of hypocrisy. Peter described them as "bold and arrogant," full of greed who "exploit you with stories they have made up" and "whose condemnation has long been hanging over them," men who "despise authority," have "eyes full of adultery," and "seduce the unstable" (2 Pet. 2:3–14).

The morning media reported the news that one of the most highly publicized and respected pastors in the whole world has been convicted, with his son, of embezzling millions of dollars of church funds. His son was sentenced to prison. Only the pastor's age spared him from the same fate, but his fine was in the multiple millions of dollars.

> We can finish well, no matter what we have done or where we have been.

Even as I am writing, another Christian news magazine informed us of a highly esteemed, nationally-known family counselor who was dismissed from the ministry he himself founded, because he had been found to have been living a duplicitous life of immorality.

Unfortunately, these stories are not all that unusual. A few years ago, when one of our well-known pastors in Nashville was discovered to have been having an affair with his secretary, I got on the phone immediately and called every young pastor I could think of, assuring them that this did not have to describe their own lives, that they could know a power of God through His Spirit that could overcome every temptation.

WALKING STRONG

Thank God, there are those who walk strong into old age. We can finish well, no matter what we have done or where we have been.

I correspond with a former convicted rapist who may be spending the rest of his life in prison, but he is now a cherished man of God who is impacting his fellow prisoners with the good news of Jesus.

The biblical Simeon was "righteous and devout. He was waiting for the consolation of Israel, and the Holy Spirit was upon him" (Luke 2:25). When he saw the infant Jesus in the arms of His parents, he walked over to Joseph and Mary, took Jesus into his arms, and said, "Sovereign

Lord, as you have promised, you now dismiss your servant in peace. For my eyes have seen your salvation, which you have prepared in the sight of all people, a light for revelation to the Gentiles and for glory to your people Israel" (vv. 29–32).

In other words, "Lord, I am ready to die now. I've seen the Promised One."

Simeon finished well.

Anna, an old woman who never left the Temple day and night, worshiping, fasting, praying, knew the moment she saw Jesus that He was the Promised Messiah. She erupted in praise, giving "thanks to God and spoke about the child to all who were looking forward to the redemption of Jerusalem" (2:38).

Anna finished well.

Caleb is one my heroes. He not only stood against the tidal wave of unbelief when reporting back to Moses as one of the twelve men who were sent to explore the land of Israel's inheritance, but he seems to have maintained that attitude of faith throughout his life. As an eighty-five-year-old man, he marched up to the younger Joshua and boldly, yet humbly declared, "Here I am today, eighty-five years old! I am still as strong today as the day Moses sent me out; I'm just as vigorous to go out to battle now as I was then. Now give me this hill country that the Lord promised me that day. You yourself heard then that the Anakites were there and their cities were large and fortified, but the Lord helping me, I will drive them out just as he said" (Josh. 14:10–12).

Caleb's words amuse me. I think he may have been stretching things just a bit. I seriously doubt that physically he was as vigorous and as strong as he was forty years earlier, but he was still strong in heart and soul—in spite of the fact that he had lived with a nation of unbelievers for forty years!

Another thing amuses me. Caleb knew he needed younger men to help him, and he knew how to recruit them: "I will give my daughter Acsah in marriage to the man who attacks and captures Kiriath Sepher [a neighboring town to Hebron]" (15:16).

In other words, "Yes, I told Joshua I am still strong, but I do realize that I need help from younger men."

Othniel picked up the challenge, won the battle, married Caleb's daughter, then became one of Israel's early judges.

Caleb finished well.

David had his share of failures—severe failures: adultery, murder—sins that brought devastation to his family and to the nation. But his heart kept turning back to the Lord. The psalms are filled with his heart-wrenching sobs of repentance as well as his exultant praise. Centuries later, God seems to have completely forgotten all of David's past sins when He described David as "a man after my own heart; he will do everything I want him to do" (Acts 13:22).

I like that! That Scripture fills me with joy. God forgets our past if we keep pressing in for more of Him. I, too, am "a man after God's heart." I may not yet fully have His heart, but I am "after" His heart!

David finished well.

Two of the Lord's chosen apostles also challenge me. One of them is the aged John, exiled on the island of Patmos because of his faith. We never hear one moment of complaint. He is so surrendered to the Lord in his old days that the Lord entrusts him with visitations and visions that have inspired and challenged believers through all the centuries. This saint of God was not impressed with his own importance. He is simply "your brother and companion in the suffering" (Rev. 1:9). What glory must have surrounded him in those closing days of his life! Suffering? Yes, but the glory of Jesus shone through him.

John finished well.

Who can ever forget Paul's words from the Roman jail: "For me to live is Christ, to die is gain" (Phil. 1:21). "I have learned the secret of being content in any and every situation, whether well fed or hungry, whether living in plenty or in want. I can do everything through him who gives me strength" (4:12–13).

Or those inimitable last words to Timothy: "The time has come for my departure. I have fought the good fight, I have finished the race, I have kept the faith. Now there is in store for me the crown of righteousness, which the Lord, the righteous Judge, will give to me on that day – and not only to me, but also to all who have longed for his appearing" (2 Tim. 4:6–9).

Paul finished well.

I want to finish well. I want to be a Paul, a John, a Simeon, an Anna, a Caleb, a David. When it's my time to go, I want to be able to look into the face of the Lord and say, "Thank You, Lord. You have led me and refined me and protected me and allowed me to participate with You in Your purpose for this generation. I have finished what You called me to do. I am ready to go."

And in the meantime, I don't ever want to forget: He works everything—*everything* for my good!

APPENDIX A

A GENTILE OBSERVANCE OF THE PASSOVER

Passover (*Pesach*) is one of "the Lord's appointed feasts" (Lev. 23:4) that still has profound prophetic implications for believers. Gather the family together on the evening of the 14th day of *Nisan* (also called "*Aviv*") on the biblical calendar, and remember that this day is the actual anniversary of Israel's deliverance from Egypt, and also the anniversary of Jesus' death.

Feel the freedom to use a *Haggadah* (meaning "the telling") if you like, but freedom in the Spirit and remembering the biblical accounts of Israel's deliverance and of Jesus' death as the Lamb of God is more important than style or tradition.

Read aloud or tell the story of Passover from Exodus 12 (abbreviated version: 12:1–14, 21–42), and make the applications for our day.

Read aloud or tell the story of Jesus as reflected in John 1:29; Luke 22:14–20; 1 Corinthians 5:7–8; 11:23–26, and pause to be grateful for Jesus, the Lamb that was slain for our deliverance.

Traditional Passover tables have a lamb bone to remember the sacrifice, "bitter herbs" (horseradish) for remembering the bitterness of slavery, parsley to be dipped in salt water in memory of the tears shed, and *charoset*, a mixture of apples, nuts and sweet wine, to remind us of the sweetness of hope in the midst of great suffering.

Unleavened bread reminds us to be ready to depart at any time, since Israel did not have time for the bread to rise. Wine will always point to the blood of Jesus.

Enjoy the meal! Remember! Rejoice!

During the meal, lead conversations about our own deliverance from the slavery of sin into the joy and freedom of Messiah Jesus. This is also a good time for testimonies of God's goodness.

Sometime during the evening, read "Remember This Day!"

REMEMBER THIS DAY!

*On this day, 3500 years ago, lambs were slaughtered throughout
Goshen in Egypt.
Hyssop brushes stroked Jewish doorposts with lamb's blood.
The children of Israel met quietly,
Sequestered behind their blood-stained doors,
Waiting to be delivered from 400 years of slavery.*

*On this night, 3500 years ago, the Lord went through the land,
looking for blood on doorposts.
There was a great deliverance, a passing-over.
Firstborn sons were slain in houses where there was no blood.
Wailing and mourning was heard when judgment came in Egypt.*

*On this night, 3500 years ago, freedom was proclaimed in Israel.
Firstborn sons of Israel were spared through the blood of the lamb.
Lamb's blood painted on doorposts brought freedom.
The wealth of Egypt became the wealth of Israel.
Shouts of joy were heard as Moses led Israel out of Egypt.*

*On this night, 3500 years ago, the exodus from Egypt came suddenly.
For 3500 years, believers in God have remembered this night.*

*On this day, 2000 years ago, another Lamb was slain.
Human hearts were stroked with Lamb's blood
And freed from centuries of slavery.*

*On this day, 2000 years ago, the Lord began to look for Lamb's
blood on the doorposts of human hearts.
There was a great deliverance, a passing-over.*

*On this day, 2000 years ago, wealth was restored to the sons of Adam.
Another Moses led another Israel out of another Egypt.*

On this day, 2000 years ago, Lamb's blood on the
doorposts of hearts brought freedom.

Today...Lamb's Blood is still found on human hearts.
Deliverance is found behind a blood-stained door.

If the doorpost of your heart is stained with Lamb's Blood,
Have a glorious Passover season.
If not, grab quickly the hyssop and look for the Lamb's blood!

The exodus will come quickly, and we will be ushered into
a whole new glorious future.

The slain Lamb has risen and will return as
King of kings and Lord of lords!

APPENDIX B

Joseph Henry Thayer's *Greek-English Lexicon of the New Testament* gives the definition of the Greek word θλιψις (*thlipsis*) as: "pressing, pressing together, pressure, oppression, affliction, tribulation, distress, straits."

Fourteen times in the NIV translation, the word is translated "trouble(s)":

Matt. 13:21; Mark 4:17 when "trouble"...comes
John 16:33 In this world you will have "trouble"
Acts 7:10 rescued him from all his "troubles"
Rom. 2:9 "trouble" and "distress" for every human being who does evil
Rom. 8:35 "trouble" or "hardship" or "persecution"
1 Cor. 7:28 those who marry will face many "troubles"
2 Cor. 1:4 comforts us in all our "troubles"
2 Cor. 4:17 our light and momentary "troubles"
2 Cor. 6:4 As servants of God, we commend ourselves.... in "troubles"
2 Cor. 7:4 in all our "troubles" my joy knows no bounds
Phil. 1:17 supposing that they can stir up "trouble" for me
Phil. 4:14 it was good of you to share in my "troubles"
2 Thess. 1:6 [God] will pay back "trouble" to those who "trouble" you

Seven times, the word is translated "distress":

Matt. 24:21; Mark 13:19 there will be great "distress", unequaled
Matt. 24:29; Mark 13:24 immediately after the "distress" of those days
2 Cor. 2:4 wrote you out of great "distress"
1 Thess. 3:7 in all our "distress" and "persecution" we were encouraged
James 1:27 visit widows in their "distress"

Seven times, the word is translated "suffering(s)":

Acts 7:11 famine struck all Egypt...bringing great "suffering"
Rom 5:3 (2x) rejoice in our "sufferings"

Eph. 3:13 not to be discouraged because of my "sufferings"
1 Thess. 1:6 in spite of severe "suffering"
Rev. 1:9 companion in the "suffering"
Rev. 2:22 will cast [Jezebel] on a bed of "suffering"

Three times, as "hardship(s)":
Acts 14:22 go through many "hardships" to enter the kingdom of God
Acts 20:23 Holy Spirit warns me that prison and "hardships" are facing me
2 Cor. 1:8 the "hardships" we suffered

Twice, as "trial(s)":
2 Cor .8:2 Out of the most severe "trial"
1 Thess. 3:3 that no one would be unsettled by these "trials"

Three times, as "affliction(s)":
Rom. 12:12 patient in "affliction"
Col. 1:24 fill up...what is still lacking in...Christ's "affliction"
Rev. 2:9 I know your "afflictions"

Four times, as "persecution(s)":
Acts 11:19 scattered by the "persecution"
2 Thess. 1:4 we boast about your perseverance...in..."persecutions"
Heb. 10:33 you were publicly exposed to insult and "persecution"
Rev. 2:10 you will suffer "persecution" for ten days

Once. as "tribulation":
Rev. 7:14 they who have come out of The Great "Tribulation"

Once, as "anguish":
John 16:21 when her baby is born she forgets the "anguish"

Once, as "hard pressed":
2 Cor. 8:13 others...relieved while you are "hard pressed"

APPENDIX C

Two Greek words are translated "wrath" in our Bibles: *thumos* (θυμος) and *orge* (οϱγη). The King James Version translates *thumos* as "wrath" 15 times; "fierceness," twice, and "indignation," once. *Orge* is translated "wrath" 31 times; "anger," 3 times; "indignation," once, and "vengeance," once. The following shows the translations in the New International Version. The important thing is that believers are protected from the wrath of God.

Matt. 3:7 (and Luke 3:7) Who warned you to flee from the coming wrath *(orge)*?

Mark 3:5 [Jesus] looked around at them in anger *(orge)*

Luke 4:28 All the people in the synagogue were furious *(thumos)* when they heard this

Luke 21:23 [Jesus, predicting the future] great distress in the land and wrath *(orge)* against this people

John 3:36 whoever rejects the Son…God's wrath *(orge)* remains on him

Acts 19:28 When [Paul's hearers] heard this, they were furious *(thumos)* and began shouting

Rom. 1:18 the wrath *(orge)* of God is being revealed from heaven

Rom. 2:5 [those who are disobedient are] storing up wrath *(orge)* against yourself for the day of God's wrath *(thumos)*

Rom. 2:8 those who… reject the truth… wrath *(orge)* and anger *(thumos)*

Rom. 3:5 If our unrighteousness brings out God's righteousness more clearly, what shall we say? That God is unjust in bringing his wrath *(orge)*

Rom. 4:15 law brings wrath *(orge)*

Rom. 5:9 [believers are]…saved from God's wrath *(orge)*

Rom. 13:4 [The governing authority] is God's servant, an agent of wrath *(orge)*

Rom. 13:5 necessary to submit to the authorities, not only because of possible punishment *(orge)*

2 Cor. 12:20 [Paul fears that when he comes, he may find] quarreling, jealousy, outbursts of anger *(thumos)*

Gal. 5:20 The acts of the sinful nature are obvious: sexual immorality, impurity...fits of rage *(thumos)*

Eph. 2:3 [We are] by nature objects of wrath *(orge)*

Eph. 4:31 Get rid of all bitterness, rage *(thumos)* and anger *(orge)*

Eph. 5:6 because of such things God's wrath *(orge)* comes on those who are disobedient

Col. 3:6 because of these, the wrath *(orge)* of God is coming

Col. 3:8 Rid yourselves of all such things as these: anger *(orge)*, rage *(thumos)*

1 Thess. 1:10 Jesus, who rescues us from the coming wrath *(orge)*

1 Thess. 2:16 The wrath *(orge)* of God has come upon them at last

1 Thess. 5:9 God did not appoint us to suffer wrath *(orge)*

1 Tim. 2:8 men everywhere to lift up holy hands in prayer, without anger *(orge)*

Heb. 3:11 I declared on oath in my anger *(orge)*

Heb. 4:3 I declared on oath in my anger *(orge)*

Heb. 11:27 By faith [Moses] left Egypt, not fearing the king's anger *(thumos)*

James 1:19 slow to become angry *(orge)*

James 1:20 man's anger *(orge)* does not bring about the righteous life

Rev. 6:16 hide us from the face of him who sits on the throne and from the wrath *(orge)* of the lamb

Rev. 6:17 The great day of (God's) wrath *(orge)* has come

Rev. 11:18 The nations were angry, and your wrath *(orge)* has come

Rev. 12:12 [The devil] is filled with fury *(thumos)*

Rev. 14:8 Fallen is Babylon the Great, which made all the nations drink the maddening *(thumos)* wine of her adulteries

Rev. 14:10 wine of God's fury *(thumos)*...cup of his wrath *(orge)*

Rev. 14:19 The angel swung his sickle on the earth, gathered its grapes and threw them into the great winepress of God's wrath *(thumos)*

Rev. 15:1 seven angels with the seven last plagues – last, because with them God's wrath *(thumos)* is complete.

Rev. 16:1 Then I heard a loud voice from the temple saying to the seven angels, 'Go, pour out the seven bowls of God's wrath *(thumos)* on the earth'

Rev. 16:19 God remembered Babylon the Great and gave her the cup filled with the wine of his fury *(thumos)* of his wrath *(orge)*

Rev. 18:3 For all the nations have drunk the maddening *(thumos)* wine of [her] adulteries

Rev. 19:15 He treads the winepress of the fury *(thumos)* of the wrath *(orge)* of God Almighty

APPENDIX D

FINTO BIBLE READING PLAN

I have tried all kinds of Bible reading plans. You probably have, too.

I tried the plan that requires you to carry a reading outline folded in your Bible to check off each chapter as you read. I always lost the paper before the year was up.

Five Psalms a day and one chapter of Proverbs will enable you to complete those books in a month. But as rich as they are, I need more than the Psalms and Proverbs. I want to get to the Gospels, the letters, the history, the prophets.

Three chapters a day every day and five on Sunday will take you through the Bible in a year. But who of us is ever sure to read three to five chapters every day? Besides, I don't like to stay in the Old Covenant Scriptures so long without reading the Gospels, Acts and the letters, and there are times when I need to read slowly so that I can meditate more thoroughly on what I am reading.

So I finally came up with a plan of my own. I never fall behind, and I never get ahead. I read as slowly or as rapidly as I wish. The only thing I need is one particular Bible for reading, and a pen or pencil to mark the last place read. I put a small number "5" for 2015, "6" for 2016, and so on, following the last portion read. The next time I read in that section, I begin where I left off, but if I should miss a day, I am not behind. If I get carried away and read all 66 chapters of Isaiah or all 28 chapters of Matthew in one day, I am not ahead.

For my reading purposes, I think of the Bible as five sections:

1. The historical section from Genesis to Esther
2. The poetic books of Job, Psalms, Proverbs, Ecclesiastes, and Song of Solomon
3. The Prophets – Isaiah to Malachi
4. The Gospels and Acts
5. Romans through Revelation

Why is this a good plan? Because I stay in all sections of Scripture at all times. If I were starting today, and if I could read as many as five chapters, I would begin with Psalm 1 (I would read Job later!). Then I would read Genesis 1, Isaiah 1, Matthew 1, and Romans 1. At the end of each of those chapters, I would put my small number designating the year. If I finish one of the sections, I simply start over in that section and "double mark" it as I continue my reading through both Old and New Covenant Scriptures at all times.

Having read the Bible regularly since early adulthood, I am still amazed to find fresh revelation during this daily time with the Lord.

WHAT DO WE DO?

OUR HISTORY

Caleb Company was started by Don Finto in 1996 as he was leaving the pastorate of Belmont Church in Nashville, TN. He named it Caleb Company because, like the biblical Caleb, Don wanted to raise up a company of warriors who would have "a different spirit" and who would follow the Lord "wholeheartedly" all their lives, who would raise up "descendants" who "will inherit the land," and to challenge old people to keep taking their mountains even into old age.

After serving in leadership with Youth With A Mission for fourteen years, Tod McDowell relocated his family to Nashville, Tennessee in 2007 to work full-time with Caleb Company. In 2010, Don shifted his role to serve as Caleb's President and Tod became Executive Director. During this transition season, we have grown into a thriving local community with team of staff, interns, and alumni focused on fulfilling the Caleb vision.

WWW.CALEBCOMPANY.ORG

TRAINING SCHOOLS

We want to raise up a generation of leaders like Caleb and Joshua who live with wholehearted devotion to Jesus, embrace God's heart for Israel and its relationship to world revival, and are released to passionately pursue their calling and destiny guided by clear personal vision rooted in biblical identity.

TOURS

Our annual Israel Tour is a powerful opportunity to experience the sights and history throughout the land of Israel while staying in excellent hotels and riding in a comfortable bus with professional guide and driver. Don and Tod personally lead this tour introducing participants to the rich relationships they have cultivated in the land.

SPEAKING MINISTRIES

We have spoken in dozens of conferences, training schools, churches and seminaries across the United States and around the world: Israel, Lebanon, Philippines, Ethiopia, Egypt, Kenya, Uganda, Mozambique, South Africa, South Korea, Singapore, Ukraine, Spain, Poland, Finland, Germany, Austria, Cyprus, France, Australia, New Zealand, Netherlands, Norway, Switzerland, Italy, Turkey, Brazil, Argentina, Mexico, England, and Canada.

CREATING RESOURCES

BOOKS, STUDY GUIDES, TRAINING MANUALS, AUDIO AND VIDEO PRODUCTS

The resources we created that further our mission include two books, *Your People Shall Be My People* and *God's Promise and the Future of Israel*. *Your People Shall Be My People* is now in sixteen languages distributed around the world. The translations are: Arabic, English, German, French, Dutch, Norwegian, Icelandic, Italian, Turkish, Spanish, Portuguese, Russian, Korean, Mandarin Chinese, Farsi, and Finnish. *God's Promise and the Future of Israel* is translated into English, German, French, Dutch, and Mandarin Chinese. We also have produced Training School Manuals, Audio and Video Recordings, and a Study Guide for the book, *Your People Shall Be My People*.

CALEB PUBLICATIONS

"PRODUCING WEAPONS OF MASS INSTRUCTION"

FOR BOOKS, EBOOKS, AND RESOURCES VISIT US AT

WWW.CALEBPUBLICATIONS.ORG

TEACHINGS · STUDY